To Bee or Not To Bee:

An Exploration of the Life and Times of the Honey Bee

Anastasia Bake

NELSON

NELSON

For permission to use material
from this text or product, submit
all requests online at
cengage.com/permissions.
Further questions about
permissions can be emailed to
permissionrequest@cengage.com

ISBN-13: 978-0-17-684210-9
ISBN-10: 0-17-684210-1

Consists of Original Works:

To Bee or Not To Bee
Anastasia Bake

Cover Credit:

De Protasov AN/Shutterstock

"Handle a book as a bee does a flower, extract its sweetness but do not damage it."
~ John Muir (1838-1914) ~

Greetings from the Hive!

What's up with all the Bee Buzz? Well the fact is bees have much to teach us, and their significance to human society is immeasurable. But even before we pull back the curtain to illuminate the honey bee's

life, let's simply start by declaring ~ *Bees are Fascinating* ~, and without the bee, life on planet Earth would not be the same.

If you have a curious mind, consider yourself an environmentalist, wildlife and nature lover, or even a gardener who *digs* the world around you, the topics explored in this text will provide a wide-ranging overview of key subjects chosen to nurture your understanding of *The Life and Times of the Honey Bee*. It will explore the honey bees caste, society and anatomy, its relationship with plants, because together they provide one-third of all the food we eat, plus, pollination is big business. Throughout the aforementioned, the individuals who have collectively advanced our knowledge will also be highlighted.

An additional overarching goal of this text is to provide you with some essential knowledge to awaken your spirit to the honey bee's plight. It is often through our concern and compassion for the well-being of others that we become inspired to act. Perhaps in time the collective voice of thousands will ensure the honey bee's survival is protected.

Human compassion can be nurtured through awareness; as such this text will begin with Chapter One: An Overview of the History of Honey Bees and Human Society. Chapter Two welcomes you to the hive, as you explore The Honey Bee's Life Cycle and you meet its Castes of Characters. Chapter Three digs a bit deeper as you will study the honey bee anatomy. Chapter 4: Flower Power, examines plants, pollination and fertilization. Chapter 5 presents an overview of beekeeping; big and small. Chapter 6 explores social justice advocacy, which might just inspired you to become an ally or activist!

To conclude, I hope you find the honey bee to be a captivating creature, and whose value will encourage you to reflect deeper and discover how you could participate in its world. I became enraptured many years ago, and I hope you too will join the club, and *bee-come*, a Bee Enthusiast!

Bee Well,
A Bake; Bee Enthusiast

Photo Credit: AnatolyM/Thinkstock

Table of Contents

Chapter 1: A Historical Look at the Relationship between the Honey Bee and Human Society

- CHAPTER OBJECTIVES
- The Historical Relationship between Humans and the Honey Bee ~ Just how far back does it go?
- The Hunt for Honey; *harvesting*
- North American Beekeeping
- Lorenzo Lorraine Langstroth
  - Chapter Review Questions, Activity, Key Terms

Chapter 2: Welcome to the Hive ~ The Honey Bee Life Cycle, Society & Behaviour

- CHAPTER OBJECTIVES
- The Honey Bee's Life Cycle ~ From Egg to Adult Bee
- Let's Meet the Casts of Characters
- The Mating Flight: Not for the weak of heart
- Colony Swarming, Supersedure, and Queenlessness
  - Chapter Review Questions, Activity, Key Terms

Chapter 3: The Anatomy of the Honey Bee ~ *The Apis mellifera*

- CHAPTER OBJECTIVES
- The Honey Bee Head, Thorax and Abdomen
- The Internal and External Structures of the Honey Bee
- The Honey Bee Exocrine Glands
- Digestive and Excretory Systems
  - Chapter Review Questions, Activity, Key Terms

Chapter 1:
A Historical Look at the Relationship Between the Honey Bee and Human Society

"The men of experiment are like the ant; they only collect and use. But the bee...gathers its materials from the flowers of the garden and of the field, but transforms and digests it by a power of its own."

~ Leonardo da Vinci (1452 – 1519) ~

CHAPTER OBJECTIVES

After reading this chapter you should be able to:

1. Describe the historical relationship between humans and the honey bee
2. Summarize the history of apiculture (beekeeping)
3. Identify key apiarists and their contributions

Introduction

The relationship between humans and the honey bee has been recorded since ancient times. Today bees are studied from divergent perspectives, including: **apiculture**, behavioural ecology, **entomology** and agriculture to name only a few. Many are also inquisitively fueled by a passion for gardening and an appreciation and respect for nature. Whatever flight pattern you traveled that steered you to open this book, chances are you have either been intrigued by these whimsical creatures, or humbled by the critical contributions they make to the overall well-being of our health, economy and environment. As Albert Einstein profoundly wrote, "if the bee disappeared off the face of the earth, man would only have four years left to live".

The human-bee duo is not the only partnership of historical significance. For millions of years bees have been evolving with flowering plants. When pollen became attached to the bees' body in their search of food, they unintentionally became the agents of pollination as they transferred pollen to the plant's female organs. At that moment, bees and plants became intimately connected (Buchmann, 2005; Seeley, 2010; Wilson-Rich, 2014). Eventually the pollinator relationship for both plants and bees became more and more specialized. Plants benefited by increased pollination, and the bees were helped to ensure a better and varied food supply to attract pollinators. Some plants even developed specialized organs; nectaries, which secret a sugary nectar at the base of the flower. This proved to be an adaptive advantage since the nectar; their main food source became an additional enticement for other types of bees. The details of the pollination process will be discussed in in Chapter 4: Flower Power.

While there are approximately 20,000 bee species that play a role in the pollination process, only seven are responsible for creating the world's sweetest treat (Seeley, 2010; Wilson-Rich, 2014). As a consequence, throughout time the honey bee has been honoured and treasured by humans. To begin our knowledge **foraging** quest, we commence by exploring the historical relationship between humans and the **Apis mellifera**, and the key individuals who furthered our knowledge and enriched our fascination.

The Historical Relationship between Humans and the Honey Bee
Just how far back does it go?

Beekeeping is as old as written history and probably much older. Evidence exists signifying human society's fondness of the stinging Apis mellifera, and studying and recording it is not new either. Cave paintings dating as far back as 15,000 years ago reveal that primitive honey hunters were documenting bees and their behaviour (Bloch et. al., 2010; Buchmann, 2005). For instance, in Valencia, Spain there is an 8000-year-old cave painting in the Mesolithic Cueva de la Araña rock shelter that has a depiction of a man climbing a ladder to get to the bees (See Illustration 1.1: The "Man of Bicorp" holding onto lianas to gather honey from a beehive).

Illustration 1.1: The "Man of Bicorp" holding onto lianas to gather honey from a beehive
● SPAIN - CIRCA 1975: stamp printed by Spain, shows Gathering honey, Arana Cave
Credit: rook76/Shutterstock

As we geographically move eastward toward Northern Africa and Eastern Europe, Seeley (2010) noted that, "solid evidence of beekeeping comes from Egypt around 2400 BC, and consists of a stone bas-relief in a temple that depicts peasants removing honeycomb from a stack of cylindrical clay hives and also packing the honey in pots (p. 44). A further historical discovery was at the Tel Rehov in the Jordan Valley of northern Israel. This location represents one of the largest ancient city mounds in Israel. It was here where scientists unearthed the remains of the oldest known honey production facility, dating back to the Iron Age (10th–early 9th centuries B.C.E.). At this site a large facility of unfired clay cylinders contain the remains of not only honey, but pollen, honey bee drones, workers, pupae, and larvae (Bloch et. al., 2010; Buchmann, 2005). Records indicate that this ancient **apiary** kept at least 75 and possibly as many as 200 hives, suggesting that at one time more than 1 million bees were housed in this location (Bloch et. al., 2010).

In **antiquity** the honey bee was revered as knowledge of its life-affirming gifts flourished. The positive impact honey and beeswax had on their economy and medicinal use also fostered this diminutive creature's exalted status as a Goddess. The ancient Egyptians experienced physical injuries, infections and some of the same medical concerns that people do today. For instance, over 700 health remedies written in hieroglyphics are described in The Ebers Papyrus (circa 1552 BC), and many of these medicines and ointments contained honey (Buchmann, 2005). The Papyrus also provided a detailed prescription for contraception which included a gummy mixture made of honey and sodium carbonate combined with crocodile dung that would be applied to the inside of the vagina ~ to cover the "mouth of the womb" (cervix). While shocking by today's standards, this concoction could be viewed as a creative forerunner of today's contraceptive sponge (Carroll, 2017; McKay et. al., 2015).

Applying honey to open wounds was another popular treatment. Based on today's knowledge this was a rational remedy considering honey's known antibacterial and fungicidal qualities (Mandal & Mandal, 2011; Molan, 1997). Harvesting honey was therefore essential. An illustration found on a wall of The Theban tomb of Pabasa portrays what most believe to be a depiction of how to evacuate a beehive. Smoke was blown into the back of the hive and the bees escaped through the entrance in the front. Also found in this tomb were as many as 500 clay cylindrical style types of bee-hives, dating back to the 7th century BC (Brodrick, 1972; Crane, 1999). The tomb of Pabasa is one of several graves located in the Valley of the Kings and Queens in Egypt, or more commonly referred to as Tombs of the Nobles (Mazar & Panitz-Cohen, 2007). Since their Gods desired sweet things, archeologists have also unearthed honey in the homes of the Pharaohs, and in jars of the grave goods of pharaohs such as Tutankhamun. Honey incidentally wasn't the only product they valued; they would also use beeswax in the mummification process (Buchmann, 2005). Additionally, throughout time the honey based beverage **mead** was enjoyed not only in ancient Egypt, but all around the globe.

Mead ~ Honey Wine

Honey and beeswax were not the only prized goods produced by bees. Mead ~ a honey-based alcoholic drink has a rich history from many lands and civilizations (Young, 1966). Mead references are scattered throughout history and literature, and even Greek philosopher Plato mention it in his writings. Examples of more recent and familiar works appear in popular fiction and their subsequent movie adaptions. You might have read and recall a verse authored by R.R. Tolkien in, *The Fellowship Of the Ring*, "The years have passed like swift droughts of sweet mead in lofty halls beyond the west" (1954). Tolkien (1937), would also reference mead in *The Hobbit*, "they sat long at the table, with their wooden drinking bowls filled with mead". And in more recent times a passage in *Harry Potter and the Half-Blood Prince,* states, "A third twitch of the wand, and a dusty bottle and five glasses appeared in mid-air. The bottle tipped and poured a generous measure of honey coloured liquid into each of the glasses, which then floated to each person in the room. "Madam Rosmerta's finest oak-matured mead," said Dumbledore, raising his glass to Harry, who had caught ahold of his own and sipped. He never tasted anything like it before, but enjoyed it immensely" (Rowling, 2009, p. 48). Although we consider wine to have had a significant place historically in human society, which includes many socio-religious functions, mead, was in fact the earliest form of wine (Vencl, 1991).

Mead can be traced back to the African bush (Young, 1966). More than 20,000 years ago feral honey bees (wild) made their hives in trees or hollow stumps. These wild colonies would be discovered by various animals that would dislodge, rob, break, and leave the unwanted comb and its honey contents on the ground. Extreme conditions of drought during the dry season, and rains in the rainy season would follow. Low sugar content syrups such as nectar would experience spontaneous fermentation as a result of the action of wild yeasts living on its skin (Maisto et al., 2013). Water + Honey + Yeast + Time... *viola* ~ mead is born. Indeed most peoples who encountered the process of fermentation probably happily tried to reproduce it (without understanding it). Over time people probably learned which sources of sugar fermented in which environments tasted best and there arose people skilled in reproducing the best drink. Eventually mead production became well known and proficient in Europe, India and China. The oldest carefully prepared mead was created on the Island of Crete. Mead was considered the drink of the Golden Age, because during this historical period, peace, harmony, stability, and prosperity prevailed, and people did not have to work to feed themselves, for the earth provided food in abundance (Heinberg, 1989). In fact the word used for drunk in classical Greek remained "honey-intoxicated".

Fun Fact: Interestingly, the word "honeymoon" in English is allegedly traceable back to the 5th century, and the practice of a bride's father dowering her with enough mead for a month-long celebration in honour of the marriage. Back then, a newlywed couple drank mead (the "honey") during their first moon of marriage. Mead was also believed to have **aphrodisiac** properties.

Polish mead was very popular in Northern Europe, and it was a desired drink among the Polish-Lithuanian nobility. It was produced by monks whose monasteries were in surroundings unfit to grow grapes. As Ian Hornsey (2003) wrote in *The History of Beer and Brewing*, the monks themselves also indulged in mead, "The dining tables had an abundance of exquisite cookery, and so much fine wine (charet), and mead, mulberry juice and other strong liquors that there was no room for ale, even though the best were made in England" (p. 289). In time, as societies became urbanized the interests and making of mead faded in popularity, and particularly once wine imports became economical.

In addition to producing mead, the Christian monasteries and convents were also centers for beekeeping. Among the many yields produced through the honey bee's handiwork, beeswax was highly prized for making candles; an essential requirement for their monasteries since beeswax did not create soot or blacken the walls when it burned. Life within the monastery would significantly change at the beginning of England's Reformation period (1536 - 1541), when English **apiculture** centers were closed by Henry VIII. The Reformation was a legal process that occurred when England broke away from the Roman Catholic Church when the Pope would not grant Henry VIII a divorce because he was a Roman Catholic. The Catholic faith believed in marriage for life and it did not recognize or support divorce. Henry responded by decreeing himself Supreme Head of the Church by an Act of Parliament in 1534. This enactment caused the dispersal of beekeeping monks, since the new protestant faith had less interest and use for candles (Buchmann, 2005). Throughout the country over 800 religious houses were effected, as they were virtually in every English town and provided the homes for monks, nuns, canons and friars. Just imagine the amount of hives that were also displaced as a result of the King's edict (Ross, 2015).

In time beekeeping would be embraced by the British Royal Families. Illustration 1.2 is a political cartoon of Prince Albert and Queen Victoria at their royal apiaries. From 1837, until her death in 1876, Queen Victoria was the reigning queen of England. It was also during this time period, when in 1874, The British Beekeepers Association (BBKA) was instituted. Their moto was "For the Encouragement, Improvement and Advancement of Bee Culture in the United Kingdom.

Fun Fact: Today's Queen Elizabeth also has beehives in her garden at Buckingham Palace, and the Queen is said to enjoy the honey from the hives as part of her breakfast each day (Wilkes, 2011).

The honey bee and human civilization experience has been chronicled throughout history. An important quantity and quality of

our present day knowledge has been the result of the shared communication of thoughts and opinions made available through literature and the arts. Even Sherlock Holmes, the most famous detective who ever lived (fictional that is), kept bees. But long before Conan Doyle was writing his mystery novels other significant historical works and artifacts were produced that have enhanced our knowledge. They can be reviewed in Chart 1.1: An Overview of Historical Contributions.

Illustration 1.2: Prince Albert and Queen Victoria at Royal Apiaries
Credit: Photos.com/Thinkstock

Chart 1.1: An Overview of Historical Contributions	
Region	**Topics of Interest**
Prehistoric Greece Crete & Mycenae	There existed a system of high-status apiculture • Beekeeping was a highly valued trade performed by beekeeping overseers ➢ Owners of gold rings depicting apiculture scenes were valued rather than previously desired religious themes
Ancient Greece	• 367 BC–347 B.C.; Aspects of the lives of bees and beekeeping are discussed at length by ancient Greek philosopher and scientist Aristotle
China	In the book *Golden Rules of Business Success* • Written by Fan Li (or Tao Zhu Gong) who was born in 517 B.C. ➢ Describes the art of beekeeping, stressing the importance of the quality of the wooden box used and how it would influence the quality of the honey
Baghdad	The Tacuinum Sanitatis ~ An 11th century Arab medical treaty • Written by Ibn Butlan of Baghdad; The work details the beneficial and harmful properties of foods and plants, which included honey
Sources: Buchmann, 2005; Bignami, 2007; Readicker-Henderson, 2009; Roberson, 2016	

Scientific events would stimulate further interest in the honey bee. By 1642, Galileo had developed an occhiolino (the word microscope was not coined by Giovanni Faber until the following year). With this new technology Italian scientists and naturalists Francesco Stelluti and Federico Cesi used it to facilitate the first and never-before-seen anatomical illustration of the structures of bees (described in their 1625 text Apiarium). This also marked the first published microscopic discovery. Seeking the approval of a powerful patron, they chose bees as their first illustration to honour Cardinal Maffeo Barberini. Their three bee diagram mimicked the Barberini family's coat-of-arms. Moreover, Barberini was also Galileo's friend, and a member of one of Italy's oldest and noblest families; the Barberini (Grens, 2015). Originally the Barberini's family coat-of-arms featured three horseflies set against a sky-blue background, but in the early 1600s, Cardinal Barberini elected to introduce a touch of elegance, and the horseflies were replaced with the honey bees. Later on August 6, 1623, Cardinal Maffeo Barberini was elected Pope Urban VIII (See Diagram 1.1: Microscopic Anatomy of Insect.

Later, when Cardinal Barberini was elected Pope Urban VIII, to win the Pope's approval many other people around him were motivated to take action. For instance, Gianlorenzo Bernini (a famous baroque architect) personally sculpted three beautiful bees in honour of the Papal's coat-of-arms on the colonnades of St Peter's Basilica in Rome, and, on the Barberini Palace. Even by today's standards, the bees are so realistically formed one might think they could fly away. And it wasn't just the artisans who sought the Pope's approval, a swarm of poets and intellectuals continually followed Pope Urban, and they were themselves described as bees.

Diagram 1.1: Microscopic Anatomy of Insect.
Francesco Stelluti and Federico Cesi first and never-before-seen anatomical illustration of the structures of bees, Rome, 1630
Credit: Gettyimages

Beekeeping in the 16th century and Onward ~ The Hunt for Honey

Many artistic renderings, such as sculpture, poetry and paintings exists confirming the fact that not only were honey bees and their products prized, but so too were the moments and activities recounting the harvest. For instance, the Renaissance was a period in European history, (14th to the 17th century), regarded by historians as the cultural bridge between the Middle Ages and modern history (de la Croix & Tansey, 1980). During this time one particular famous artist, Pieter Bruegel the

Elder (Netherlandish, approx., 1569), portrayed the honey harvest in pen and brown ink, called *The Beekeepers*.

German Renaissance painter and printmaker Lucas Cranach the Elder (1525) would express a moral narrative in his painting called, 'Cupid complaining to Venus', (See Photo Image 1. 1: Cupid complaining to Venus'). The legend being articulated describes the story of humans and bees, as it illustrates Cupid being stung by bees while stealing their honeycomb. This painting's declaration is, as the inscription observes: "life's pleasure is mixed with pain." This exquisite painting is hung in the National Gallery of England (London) to be enjoyed by all (See Photo Image 1. 1: Cupid Complaining to Venus).

Photo Image 1.1: Cupid Complaining to Venus
Painting hangs in the National Gallery of England, London.
Credit: © National Gallery, London/Art Resource, NY

Early civilizations would quickly master basic honey hunting skills. Originally, when honey was collected from wild bee colonies this wasn't really beekeeping, today it would more appropriately

be described as honey hunting or honey gathering. In this process the wild colony was spoiled or destroyed when the wax and honey were taken (See Illustration 1.3: Beekeepers Preparing to Capture a Swarm of Bees). Incidentally this form of honey harvesting still occurs in many places around the world.

In time, societies would eventually set their sights on domesticating wild bees. Perhaps we should pause and make this point crystal clear ~ honey bees are not exactly domesticated, but humans have learned how to *manage* them (Langstroth, 1860). Ongoing advancements in science and technology during the Enlightenment period (1685-1815) would continue to unfold and provide further insights into apiculture practices.

Illustration 1.3: Beekeepers Preparing to Capture a Swarm of Bees. Notice the group of skeps
Credit: Photos.com/Thinkstock

Observe Illustration 1.4: Set of Beehives. This image was published in 1897, in the Meyers Konversations-Lexikon, which was a major encyclopedia in the German language. It would continue to be published in various editions and by several titles from 1839 to 1984.

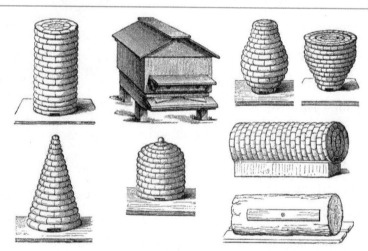

Illustration 1.4: Set of Beehives
Credit: Hein Nouwens/Shutterstock

One of the first important insights occurred when people discovered it was easier to make a *home* or hive nearby to control the environment, and thus, reduce the amount of time spent searching for wild colonies. During the next couple hundred years throughout Europe and Great Britain, an on-going commitment to advance beekeeping knowledge continued and honey bees were kept in a variety of containers around the world. Examples included; clay pots, hollowed logs, wooden boxes, and skeps (See Photo Image 1.2: Old beehives and Wooden Church).

Photo Image 1.2: Old beehives and wooden church on a meadow
In Folk Arts Museum Pirogovo, Kiev, Ukraine
Credit: Photo travel VlaD/Shutterstock

To manage honey bees the **skep** became one of the most popular and commonly used methods embraced throughout Western Europe. It is essentially a straw basket that derives its name from the Anglo-Saxon word 'skeppa' which simply means basket. Typically it was a conical formed basket made of long wheat straw coiled and stitched with blackberry briar. They also have small loops at the top to allow them to be easily lifted. This lifting or **'hefting'** was an acquired skill for judging the weight of honey inside. Even today some beekeepers might still use a skep for capturing swarms.

Photo Image 1.3: Skep
⬡ Conical basket made of long coiled straw
Credit: Suljo/Thinkstock

Although the variety of manmade hives provided a somewhat managed and safe place for bees to build their colony, make wax and honey, when it was time to harvest a common problem ensued. The honeycombs were torn out and smashed up, along with the eggs, larvae, honey, and the colony of bees would be lost. As time passed, and in more settled societies the destruction of the hive meant a loss of valuable resources. This problem made beekeeping both inefficient and somewhat of a "stop and start" endeavour. Also taking hold was the awareness that the status quo would not support the possibility of selective breeding since honey bee colonies were destroyed, along with their vital queen. But these concerns were not unnoticed and human imagination, aptitude, and inventiveness emerged.

Critical to the advancement of beekeeping was the wisdom of Johann Dzierzon, a Polish apiculturist who was born in 1811. Dzierzon would create a "revolution" in bee-culture (Langstroth, 1986, p. 21). Today he is considered the father of modern **apiology** (a branch of entomology concerning the scientific study of bees). In 1833, Dzierzon graduated from the Breslau University Faculty of Catholic Theology, and thereafter, combine his theoretical and practical work in apiculture with his duties. In his apiary, Dzierzon studied the social life of honey bees while constructing several beehives. In time he created quit a buzz, as world-wide knowledge of his innovations and discoveries became known in scientific and bee-keeping circles (Langstroth, 1860). Equally significant was Dzierzon discovery (1835) of the phenomenon of **parthenogenesis** in bees, as he recognized drones are produced from unfertilized eggs, while both queen honey bees and female worker bees were the products of fertilization. He also discovered the mechanism of secretion of royal jelly and its role in the development of queen bees.

As his research continued, in 1838 he devised the first practical movable-comb beehive which allowed manipulation of individual honeycombs without destroying the structure of the hive. Later, based on Dzierzon work, in the United States, Lorenzo Lorraine Langstroth would design his own version of a frame-movable hive (Langstroth, 1860).

In 1962 in recognition of his life's achievements, The Rev. Johann Dzierzon Museum of Apiculture was established at Kluczbork (a town in southwestern Poland). The museum focuses on Dzierzon's work and houses 5 thousand volumes of his publications regarding beekeeping. At this museum there are beehives of various shapes on display.

In 1956, a stamp was issued in Poland for the 50th death anniversary of Johann Dzierzon (Please see Illustration 1.5: Dr. Jan Dzierzon, circa 1956).

Illustration 1.5: Dr. Jan Dzierzon, circa 1956)
Credit: Lefteris Papaulakis/Shutterstock

North America Beekeeping

By the 18th and 19th centuries, European societies began to reap the rewards of a continuous transformation in beekeeping knowledge. Europeans were acquiring knowledge regarding the biology of bees, the bee colony, and the *how-to* of keeping bees. Also unfolding was the European migration to North America, and the immigrating English colonists would bring with them their extensive beekeeping skills and honey bees. It must be noted that despite the fact that there were many pollinating bees, there is no documentation to prove precisely, when, and who brought the honey bee to North America. However scarce evidence exists that would support the fact that there had been native honey bees. The general consensus however, is that the very early colonists when immigrating brought with them the honey bee, and finding the environment favourable, bees would establish colonies in the wild through swarming.

Despite the benefits and enjoyment the new sweet treat provided, there was a unique response in the late 1600s from the original inhabitants; the Native Americans to the European Honey Bee's arrival. In fact, early American writer, Thomas Jefferson, stated that the Native Americans called the honey bees "white man's flies." The name was a response to the fact that the appearance of honey bees in America was associated with the arrival of the Europeans and the continual cultural and land conflicts that would ensue for indigenous people across North America. The Cherokees however, were the first tribe to begin practicing the art of beekeeping, when they saw how bees could be induced to "work" for them.

In time as knowledge of bee management grew, the colonist would learn to manage the honey bee, and the bee's arrival would signal the beginning of honey production, and beekeeping would become a profitable livelihood. Let's now explore one key individual from the mid-1800s, and his contribution to the profession of apiary; beekeeping.

Lorenzo Lorraine Langstroth

In the mid-1800s, a new insight was gleaned that would revolutionize beekeeping. This invention allowed beekeepers to harvest their honey without terminating the entire colony. And what might you ask was this *beekeeping game changer*, and who *invented* it? Consider this question first. When you hear the name Thomas Edison what comes to mind? *The Electric light bulb*? Great, How about the name Henry Ford? Did you think… *automobile*? Okay, let's move forward, Mark Zuckerberg …. Yes of course…*Facebook*?? Hopefully by the time you finish this chapter, when you hear the name L. L. Langstroth you will think … *Father of American Beekeeping*.

Although many others contributed to our present day honey bee knowledge (See Chart 1.2: Important Individuals and their Influences: A Honey Bee Time Line), it was indeed, Lorenzo Lorraine Langstroth who revolutionized the keeping of bees. He was born in 1851 and lived in Philadelphia, Pennsylvania (See Photo Image: 1.4: Lorenzo Lorraine Langstroth First Book). He was a clergyman and an educator, but today he is mostly remembered as The "Father of American Beekeeping", and the inventor of the Langstroth hive.

Photo Image: 1.4: Lorenzo Lorraine Langstroth First Book
⬡ A Practical Treatise on the Hive and Honey-Bee
Credit: Bake

In 1853 he wrote, *The Hive and the Honey-bee: A Beekeeper's Manual*. He begins his book apprising the reader of the following:

"It is now more than twenty years since I turned my attention to the keeping of bees. The state of my health of late years have compelled me to live much in the open air, I have devoted a large portion of my time to a minute investigation of their habits, as well as to a series of careful experiments the construction and management of hives (Langstroth, 1860, p. 14).

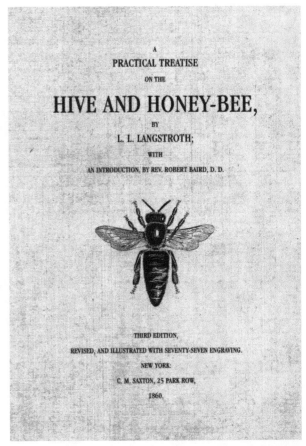

During these 20+ years Langstroth would build upon the observations of Huber and the principals of beekeeping provided by Dzierzon, who was considered to be the leading expert in apiary studies. To enhance his expertise and interest Langstroth built observation hives with glass components that made visible the internal life of the bee colony. He firmly believed a profitable system of bee-keeping could be achieved with a precise; exact, construction design. The key feature he believed was to have, "complete control of the combs, so that any or all of them would be removed at pleasure" (Langstroth, 1860, p 14).

Langstroth years spent studying, observing and experimenting with the bees would lead to his hive design, and it continues to exist today. The rectangular bee box design has removal wooden frames which allow beekeepers the opportunity to inspect, and remove honey from the honeycomb, while preventing the destruction of comb and the disturbance of the bee colony.

Key to Langstroth breakthrough and his most crucial discovery was a divergent and unique design idea. Unlike earlier forms of manmade beekeeping hives, his design left just enough wiggle room for the bees to move around in the dark in the confines of their hive. He referred to this gap as **"bee space"**, and the calculation was precise, 8 mm or 3/8 of an inch, whichever measurement you prefer. (See Photo Image 1.5: Bee Space). Moreover, this space also mimicked the natural space in the shallow chambers of a hive, so the bees would refrain from covering this area with comb or block it with bee glue, also referred to as propolis (See Chapter 2, Photo Image 2.4: Wild Beehive in the nature). Langstroth's vision and invention transformed the business of beekeeping.

Photo Image 1.5: Bees Space
- Note the frames are 8 mm apart, leaving room for the bees to come and go
- You will also note the beekeeper is using gloves for protection as the frames are maneuvered from right to left allowing them to be remove to inspect and or harvest honey.
Credit: Thinkstock/Roger Asbury

Beekeeping became commercially viable during the 19th century. Apart from the moveable-frame hive design, three additional inventions drove the industry; the smoker, the comb foundation maker, and the honey extractor. Even today, these innovations support commercial apiculture. Worldwide, those involved in beekeeping gained a method by which they could provide large crop pollination, and today it is even more crucial to agriculture. To ensure we have access to a diversity of healthy food, beekeeping must be respected and remain a viable industry. Later the queen grafting tool was developed, which enables beekeepers to control a bee's genetic line so they can produce and sell bees. which has also become a significant part of todays' apicultural business.

Chart 1.2: Important Individuals and their Influences: A Honey Bee Time Line	
Key Individual	**Contribution**
François Huber (1750 – 1831) Lived 81 years	• Swiss naturalist, who documented the following: ○ Honey bees reproduced by swarming ○ When a virgin queen emerges she is left alone to fight and kill other virgin queen and would then leave to mate and return • First to recognize that drones die after copulation
Johann Dzierzon (1811 – 1906) Lived 95 years	• Studied the social life of bees and discovered the phenomenon of **Parthenogenesis** in bees ○ Proposed that queen and female worker bees were products of *fertilization* and drones were not ○ The immature bees diets contributed to their subsequent roles • In 1838: devised the first practical movable-comb beehive ○ His design allowed the manipulation of individual honeycombs without destroying the structure of the hive
William Broughton Carr (1836–1909) Lived 73 years	• English inventor, beekeeper and writer ○ 1890: invented the WBC • Often considered to be inconvenient because it had to be dismantle ○ This hive design was a variation on the Langstroth Hive
Abbé Émile Warré (1867 – 1951) Lived 84 years	• French monk who studied and experimented with over 300 hive types ○ Ranged from Skeps to the Langstroth hive • Wanted to provide bees an experience *they* would seek out in nature ○ Advocated for less interference with hives and bees • In 1948: published "*Beekeeping For All*" ○ The book outlines plans for a top bar bee hive design
Henry Alley	• Was a 19th-century American apiarist and author • In 1861; successfully rearing queen bees Developed the Alley method of Queen-Rearing • Published: *The Bee-Keeper's Handy Book: Or Twenty-Two Years of Queen Rearing Experience Apiculturist; A Journal Devoted to Practical Beekeeping*
Gilbert M. Doolittle (1846-1918) Lived 72 years	• A 19th-century apiarist and author • In 1889: developed a comprehensive system for rearing queens • Considered to be the father of *Commercial* queen rearing • His book Scientific Queen-Rearing: As Practically Applied • His involvement coincided with the USA's expansion of apiary knowledge
Sources: Doolittle,1889; Langstroth, 1860; Mangum , 2015; Martin, 1980	

Conclusion

The commercial beekeeping industry was not the only beneficiary from Langstroth hive portability. The ease of its design has also nurtured individual passionate pursuits, and today they are incorporated into personal gardens worldwide. Beehives can also be spotted on the rooftops of large buildings in major cities and in community gardens, to be collectively shared and experience by many. And for this capability we can thank L. L. Langstroth, who is…..? Yes that is correct; The Father of American Beekeeping (See Illustration: 1.6: Yes you too can keep bees).

Illustration: 1.6: Yes you too can keep bees!
⬡ The Langstroth Hive design and a beekeeper properly dressed lifting a frame of honey
Credit: Dmitry Natashin/Shutterstock

CHAPTER REVIEW QUESTIONS

1. What is the scientific (Latin) name for the honey bee?
   a. Apium Pollanade
   b. Arnim Hocynthe
   c. Ursa Melera
   d. Apis Mellifera

2. In which country was there an archeological finding dating back to the Iron Age that provided evidenced of a large apiary facility?
   a. England
   b. Israel
   c. Greece
   d. Turkey

3. Which of the following derives its name from the Anglo-Saxon word which simply means basket?
   a. Hefter
   b. Cylinder
   c. Skep
   d. Cove

4. In what country did Lorenzo Lorraine Langstroth observe and record his findings of the honey bee?
    a. The United States
    b. Canada
    c. England
    d. Austria

5. Who would first use a microscope to facilitate a detailed drawing of bees?
    a. Johann Dzierzon
    b. Francesco Stelluti
    c. Henry VIII
    d. Abbé Émile Warré

6. Who is considered the father of commercial queen rearing?
    a. Henry Alley
    b. Johann Dzierzon
    c. Lorenzo Langstroth
    d. Gilbert M. Doolittle

7. Whose work concentrated on successfully rearing queen bees?
    a. Henry Alley
    b. Johann Dzierzon
    c. Abbé Warré
    d. Gilbert M. Doolittle

8. Who is considered the "Father of American beekeeping"?
    a. Johann Dzierzon
    b. Lorenzo Langstroth
    c. Abbé Warré
    d. Gilbert M. Doolittle

9. Who outlined in his book plans for a top bar bee hive, because it creates far less interference with and bees?
    a. Henry Alley
    b. Johann Dzierzon
    c. Abbé Warré
    d. Gilbert M. Doolittle

10. How big is the bee space?
    a. 2 mm
    b. 4 mm
    c. 6 mm
    d. 8 mm

ACTIVITY

To enhance your understanding and nurture your curiosities check out the following:

Henry Alley's book on open library
- *The bee-keeper's handy book: or Twenty-two years' experience in queen-rearing.* You can read through his book that was written in https://archive.org/details/beekeepershandyb00alle
- The American Apiculturist Journal http://www.survivorlibrary.com/library/the_american_apiculturist_vol_08_1890.pdf

François Huber's (1841). Observations on the natural history of bees
- https://archive.org/details/0048OBSE

François Huber's (1840). *The natural history of bees.*
- Comprehending the uses and economical management of the British and foreign honey-bee; together with the known wild species. Illustrated by thirty-six [i.e. thirty-two] plates coloured from nature, with portrait and memoir
- https://archive.org/details/naturalhistoryb00hubegoog

Langstroth (1853)
- On the hive and the honey-bee, a bee-keeper's manual
- https://archive.org/details/langstrothonhiv00lang

KEY TERMS

Antiquity; anˈtikwədē (an-tik-wi-tee)
- The ancient past, especially the period before the Middle Ages (also referred to as the Medieval Period)
- The peoples, nations, tribes, or cultures of ancient times
- Lasted from the 5th to the 15th century

Apiarist
- The *-ist* suffix is a Greek form that means "a person connected with"
- An individual who keeps bees, or beekeeper

Apiary
- A location where bees are kept or "bee yard"

Apiculture; Apiculture (from Latin: apis "bee")
- Is the maintenance of honey bee colonies, commonly in hives, by humans

Apiology
- A branch of entomology concerning the scientific study of bees

Aphrodisiac
- A food, drink, or drug that stimulates sexual desire

Entomology
- The branch of zoology concerned with the study of insects

Ethnography
- Is the scientific description of the customs of individual peoples and cultures

Foraging
- To search widely for food or provisions

Hefting
- The act of lifting which was an acquired skill for judging the weight (amount) of honey

Naturalist
- Experts in natural history, and study not only living things, such as plants and wildlife, but non-living things, such as minerals and fossils

Propolis
- Also called bee glue, is a resinous mixture that honey bees produce by mixing saliva and beeswax with an oozed substance, gathered from tree buds, sap flows, or other botanical sources

Chapter 1: Review and Study Notes

Chapter 1: Review and Study Notes

Chapter 1: Review and Study Notes

Chapter 2
Welcome to the Hive ~ The Honey Bee Life Cycle, Society & Behaviour

*"For so work the honey-bees, creatures that by a rule in nature teach
the act of order to a peopled kingdom."*

~ William Shakespeare (1564- 1616) ~

CHAPTER OBJECTIVES

After reading this chapter you should be able to:

1. Explain a step-by-step account of the life cycle of worker, drone, and queen bee
2. Discuss the bee's complex and sophisticated caste system
3. Describe the honey bee's mating ritual
4. Define colony swarming, supersedure, and queenlessness

Introduction

One of the most elegant, whimsical, and productive creatures existing in our gardens and in nature is the European honey bee (**Apis mellifera**). Unlike other bees, honey bees are a true social species referred to as **eusocial**. As such they possess three characteristics: cooperative brood care, there is an overlap of two or more generations with offspring assisting with the **brood**, and a reproductive division of labour (Zablotny, 2009). Moreover, within this collective and very complex social structure each bee will individually carrying out their own specialized functions (Seeley, 2010; Underwood et al., 2004). The colony is composed of a caste of three specific bees; the queen, the female worker bee and the male drone bee. In this chapter we will examine each member and the vital roles they have in safeguarding the survival of the colony. To begin we will study their life cycle, or to put it in human terms ~ the honey bee's prenatal period.

The Honey Bee's Life Cycle ~ From Egg to Adult Bee

All bees will progress through the same unfolding four stages; egg, larva, pupa and adult bee, but subtle and significant differences do unfold, as well as the time required for the each bee's development (See Chart 2.1: The Honey Bee Life Cycle). A discernment that unfolds during the bee's development is a specialty of the queen bee, because she decides which eggs will or will not be fertilized (Boes, 2009; Seeley, 2010). If an egg is fertilized a female worker bee develops, if unfertilized a male bee will emerge; a drone (Seeley, 2010; Warton et. al., 2007). Upon an even closer examination it becomes clear that the three bees also look physically dissimilar. These differences will be examined more fully in Chapter 3: The Honey Bee Anatomy.

Chart 2.1 The Honey Bee Life Cycle				
Bee	**Egg # of Days**	**Larva # of Days**	**Pupa # of Days**	**Adult # of Days**
Queen	1-3	4-9	10-15	16
Worker	1-3	4-9	10-20	21
Drone	1-3	4-9	10-23	24
Source: Bake, 2016				

Eggs

The Queen bee is the member of the colony who lays eggs and determines gender. The eggs are pearly white in colour, are of a lengthened, oval shape, with a slight curvature. In fact one might say it resembles a piece of uncooked rice. The queen usually lays one egg per **brood** cell and glues it to the floor of the cell, which gives the appearance that it is standing straight up in the center (Warton et. al., 2007). The part of the egg facing down will develop into the head and it is slightly thicker than the abdominal end. According to Blackiston (2015), eggs are about 1.7 millimeters long. The hatching of the egg into the first larva state is virtually unnoticeable (See Diagram 2.1: The Honey Bee Life Cycle). It has also been established that the worker honey bees (infertile females) regulate their colony's investment in drones because it is the workers who build the wax cells for rearing drones, and they also tend to all the developing larvae within the hive (Warton et. al., 2007).

Larva (**Larvae** is plural)

By day 3 or 4, the egg hatches into its larva stage. The larva is small and whitish; they have no eyes, legs, wings or antennae, and possess only the simple mouth parts needed to drink large quantities of food (Seeley, 2010; Winston, 1987). They are essentially feeding machines, but are otherwise quite helpless. The larva floats in white nourishment produced by, and placed in the brood cells by the nursing worker bees. So interesting is this sight that the father of modern beekeeping L. L. Langstroth wrote, "So nicely do the bees calculate the quantity of food which will be required, that none remain in the cell when it transforms to a nymph" (1860, p.44).

Photo Image 2.1: Open Brood
Notice the eggs, standing upright and placed in the center of the cell, and the various sizes of larvae
Credit: NinaHenry/Thinkstock

The final step which completes the larva stage involves capping the larva cell. Until the cell is capped it is referred to as **open brood** (See Photo Image: 2.1: Open Brood). Several worker bees may work together or even a single bee can complete the capping task by combining a wax mixture with **propolis**. Brood caps will differ in colour compared to the paler hue of the honey cell, since wax is only used to construct honey comb. Brood cap also vary in shape, for instance the drone's cap is curved, like a dome, compared to that of a worker cell that is flat in appearance (See Photo Image 2.3), and the queen cell is even more distinct, which will be described in greater detail later in this chapter.

Pupa (**Pupae** is plural)

Once the cell is capped and sealed, the larva will spin a cocoon around their body. This will be the last period before the final adult bee emerges (Langstroth, 1860; Winston, 1987). The transformations that are now taking place are hidden from sight under their capping. As the pupa develops, the **cuticle** gradually becomes darker and these well-defined colour changes can be used to determine the pupal age (Seeley, 2010). The pupa does not grow or change shape externally, but internally organ and muscle systems undergo substantial changes as their adult form including the eyes, legs, and wings take shape. The fine branch hairs that cover the bee's body are the last to develop (Seeley, 2010). Once the bee is ready to emerge they will use their **mandibles** to perorate the cell capping. The total development period ~ from laid egg until the adult bee emerges differs according to the type of honey bee. Although the hive's health and temperature may create some variance, generally the time frame is, **Queen, 16 days**; **Worker Bee, 21 days**; **Drone, 24 days** (See Illustration 2.1: The Honey Bee Life Cycle). The moment bees emerge they begin their unique contribution to the colony.

Illustration 2.1: The Honey Bee Life Cycle				
Egg	Larva	Pupa; *Capped*	Developing Pupa	Emerging Adult Bee
Credit: De NoPainNoGain/Shutterstock				

Let's Meet the Caste of Characters

The life span of every honey bee begins when an egg hatches, and the colony's survival depends upon its various bees (See Illustration 2.2: The Honey Bees). Each member of the colony has its own characteristics and specific responsibilities critical to the preservation of the hive. In a solitary state a single bee is as helpless as a new-born child. Yet, collectively bees can thrive and provide human society an estimated one third of the food we consume each day. In a colony's caste ordinarily there are just a few hundred drones and ultimately one queen in every hive. The rest of the colony is made up of worker bees, and they can be as many as 60,000 in a strong hive (Boes, 2010; Seeley, 2010). Interested to learn why? Let's Meet the Caste of Characters.

Illustration 2.2: The Honey Bees
⬤ The Queen, Drone and Worker
Source: Bake, 2015

Long Live the Queen; *Her Birth and Duties*

L. L. Langstroth wrote, "The Queen-Bee, as she is the common mother of the whole colony, may very properly be called the mother-bee. She reigns most unquestionably by a divine right, for every good mother ought to be queen in her own family" (1860, p. 30). As such, within her hive she is treated with great respect and affection by the other bees. Her every need is attended to, offering her honey from time-to-time, and backing out of her way as she moves around the comb. The potential life of every bee begins when the queen lays her egg in the **brood** cells, as she is the only female bee in the hive that has fully developed reproductive organs, as such she is referred to as a perfect female (Amdam & Omholt, 2003).

Physically the queen bee is the biggest member of the caste. Her wings are shorter than her body, and she has a long tapered abdomen that supports her egg laying duties. As her egg passes through the ovary into the oviduct she will decide whether or not a particular egg is fertilized, and this step determines sex. An unfertilized egg becomes a drone, and a fertilized egg develops into female worker. Each day the queen will lay between 1,000 and 2,000 eggs. When a young healthy queen lays eggs, she packs them closely together within the cells. As a queen ages her sperm stores will decrease, causing her to produce fewer eggs. The pattern of her laid eggs will also begin to appear less orderly. Although estimates exist regarding the length of her life span, the average is approximately 2-4 years. There have been some studies published that have even suggested that some queens have even lived as long as 8 years (Boes, 2010; Seeley, 2010).

Photo Image 2.2: Honey Bee Brood
⬡ You are looking at Langstroth's removable hive design. Notice the honey comb, and the distinctive queen cell. What else do you think is unfolding inside the hive?
Credit: iSidhe/Thinkstock

Two important decisions are made to nurture the development of a new queen bee, and these decisions are made exclusively by the workers. The first indication that a potential queen bee is developing within an existing hive can be seen within the **brood comb**, because queen cells differ starkly in appearance compared to the rest of the hive (See Photo Images 2.2 and 2.3). They are larger and designed vertically. Visually they look very similar to a peanut. This vertical design also supports the queen's development since she hangs head down (See Photo 2.2). The other variance is her diet. After an egg is laid and fertilized a future queen is fed an exclusive diet of **royal jelly** throughout her entire egg to larva period. Royal jelly is a secretion that the worker bees produce and store in their head glands. Royal jelly contains dietary supplements, fertility stimulants, as well as B vitamins (Amdam & Omholt, 2003; Tew, 2015). Similar to the worker and drone, once the larva period is completed, her brood cell will be capped.

The queen also has the shortest development, and will emerge as a full-grown bee within 16 days. When it is time for the queen to leave her cell she chews through the cap. As she chews she emits a sound that is believed to warn any other hatching queens of her arrival. For you music virtuosos, their emerging sound is very similar to G-sharp. Just for fun, or curiosity, take a moment and

google g-sharp to experience the sound. Check out the ACTIVITY section of this chapter.

Photo Image 2.3: Honey Bees at Work
⬡ Worker bees and the open brood; eggs, larvae, and capped brood cells and honey
Credit: Peter Maerky/Shutterstock

After the first virgin queen bee has hatched, it is also not unusual to find that that the additional nurtured un-emerged queen bees have slits in their brood cells. Why, because the queen bee instinctively and immediately acts to ensure her dominance; her throne, thus she will attempt to kill the other queens (Winston, 1987). However, worker bees also have a primal drive to safeguard the hive's survival and will endeavour to keep several young queens alive during this time period in the event a backup queen is needed should the first queen not survive her virginal flight. If two virgin queens should emerge simultaneously, they will fight each other to the death.

The next task of the queen is to take her virginal flight and successfully mate with at least 10 drones. Thereafter she will return to the hive and begin laying eggs. If the old queen is still alive or present within the hive, either the workers or the new queen will kill her when she returns (Seeley, 2010; Smith, 1949). Either way, the colony's survival is dependent on this new queen's ability to lay a plentitude of fertilized eggs to produce a well-developed force of worker bees for the colony. And as noted earlier, the life span and survival of a honey bee colony depends upon all its members.

As the queen goes about her egg laying task thoughtful attention is made as she examines each egg before placing it into a cell. Laying an egg takes only a few seconds and a queen can place up to 2000 eggs within a single day. If all is well in the honey hive the queen will be the longest surviving member (Seeley, 2010; Smith, 1949). When however an existing queen dies or becomes incapable of laying eggs, and many indicators exist that would signal this concern, the worker bees will begin the process of rearing a new queen to guarantee the colony's survival. Specifically they will commence the process to raise a new queen if queenlessness (emergency), supersedure (failing queen) or swarming (crowding) occurs. Before proceeding to discuss the details of these concepts, the other members of the hive will be described.

The Worker Bee

The worker bee begins its development as an egg, and for the first few days it is exclusively fed royal jelly. Unlike the queen bee, around the 4th day, while still in her larva stage her diet will change and the workers will provide a mixture of pollen and honey, a food substance referred to as bee bread. The worker is an infertile female, thus she does not produce fertilized eggs nor does she establish new colonies.

Physically the workers are the smallest members of the colony, yet they compose the bulk of the hive population. For instance, a hive can contain 20,000 to 80,000 workers, and there may only be a single queen and 100 drones. Their pre-natal development is roughly 21 days. After the worker emerges she will begin assuming a variety of duties over her life span which will be determined by her age. Thus, she might be thought of as both a generalist and specialist. The worker bee's task expectations will unfolds sequentially (Visscher, 1983; Winston, 1987). Various terms have been used to describe these roles, but the most common are, an inside worker (house bee) and outside worker. Chart 2.2: Worker Bee; From Egg to Forager, will describe the developmental timing of her various roles.

Chart 2.2: Worker Bee; From Egg to Forager	
Day	
Egg	• The egg of bee is of a lengthened, oval shape, with a slight curvature • They adhere to the base of the cell, and remain unchanged until they hatch
3-4	• Egg hatches into its larvae state; resembling a small white worm, and floats in a whitish transparent fluid, which is deposited in the cells by the nursing-bees • After her third day she is fed **bee bread**; unlike the queen who only receives royal jelly
5-21	• Capped cell and pupa stage
22	• Chews her way out of her cell and joins the colony
Inside Duties	
22-24	**Cleaner**: Cell preparation • Involves removing remains of the cocoons and larva excreta • Attends to the cells; smoothing walls removing brood caps • Cleans brood cells so more eggs can be laid
24-32	**Nurse** • Feeding and Tending to brood; larva
32-40	**Builder** • Bees secrete wax (wax plates) on their abdomen and use it to build honeycomb • Caps honey and brood cells with wax she produces
Outside Duties	
40-43	**Guard** • She has reached peak strength, is very energetic, she is ready to leave the hive • Fit to stand guard and defend the hive, which is also the point of entry of the colony's enemies
43+	**Forager and Scout** • Leaves to collect food, which includes nectar, pollen, **propolis**, and water • Looking for new nesting sites and food sources
Sources: Amdam & Omholt, 2003; Langstroth, 1860; Smith, 1949; Tew, 2015; Winston, 1987; Visscher, 1983	

Worker Bee: *From Nurse Bee to Forager*

The worker bee's contribution to the hive is significant. There is an orderly timing to all the tasks she does as she continues to grow within the hive. Worker begin their first days of life cleaning cells, and they will not leave the hive to forage for a few more weeks. A fun point to consider, if you have watched the rather entertaining *Bee Movie* (2007), this film does not present an authentic look at a honey bee's life; and yes I know it's just a movie. However, if you recall, Benson (voiced by Jerry Seinfeld) becomes disillusioned with his position at Honex Industries after his bee co-workers inform him he'll be stuck repeatedly doing the same thing over and over each and every day. As you will now appreciate, task tedium is not the worker bee's reality.

Photo Image 2.3: Young bee emerging from their brood cell
⬡ Notice the larva. Which bee do you think is in the other capped pupa cells?
⬤ After Reading Chapter 3, refer back to this image and identify the bee's anatomical parts
Credit: Vova Shevchuk/Stutterstock

The first few weeks of a worker's life are spent working within the hive (Figure 2.2). Her house duties include the role of cleaner; as she cleans out brood cells as new bees emerge. She will remove the cocoon remains, larva excreta, leftover capping, and smooth the cell walls. This provides the queen the opportunity to continually lay her eggs. Cleaning and preparing a cell typically takes a bee about 41 minutes, involving 15-30 workers (Winston, 1987). Older worker bees will remove dead bees from the hive by flying outside and discarding their corpses (Visscher, 1983).

Usually by the time the adult bee is 3 days old she begins her next role; nurse-bee. At this point she can feed brood food to the larvae since her glands are now well-developed. A single larva is tended by many nurse-bees. As her wax glands mature she will also begin producing wax from her abdomen, and begin building and capping honey and brood cells. On her 40th day she will move outside and guard the hive entrance. Soon thereafter, she will forage and generally this will be her last and final role. The worker's life span from laid egg to the death averages between 7 to 9 weeks, or as Langstroth wrote, "their age depends very much upon their greater or less exposure to injurious influences and severe labors" (1860, p. 59).

Foraging is the last development task for the honey bee. Foraging begins in the spring after a long winter in the hive. Bees get almost all their food from flowers. Attracted by a flower's sweet smell and bright colour, they are able to gather the necessary proteins and carbohydrates vital for their survival. They will suck up the sugary nectar at the base of the flower, and while foraging the protein rich pollen with gather on the hairs of their body. To save the pollen a bee will stow it away on sacs on its hind legs (See Chapter 3: The Anatomy of the Honey Bee). A bee can carry its own weight in pollen and nectar and still fly. It will consume only what is necessary for their activities, as the majority of their bounty will be shared with the hive. They will visit hundreds of blossoms a day, working as long as the sunlight last. Each time they return to the hive, the nectar they stored in their honey crop will be regurgitated and placed in honey cells. Once it has thickened and becomes honey (enough water has evaporated) it will be capped with wax (like a lid on jar), and used later when needed. Pollen in stored in separate cells, later it is mixed with honey to feed to the young. The honey and pollen cells collectively provide the necessary food for all members of the hive. The thrills, trials and tribulations of foraging will be explored in greater detail in Chapter 4: Flower Power.

The Drone

The drone bee is the male bee member in a colony, and is the product of an unfertilized egg. When he emerges from his brood cell, he will often require the assistance of the worker bees. He is the minority in number, and in the peak season his numbers may still only range from a hundred to a thousand, and recall, an average hive can be as large as 60,000 (Blackiston, 2015). He is however much larger and stronger than either the queen or workers; however his body is not quite as long as that of the queen. While a drone bee is in flight he can fly backward, rotate and flip. Yes, he is indeed somewhat of an acrobat!

A drone's **proboscis** is short so gathering nectar from flowers is not possible, nor does he have a basket on his hind legs for holding pollen, no glands on his abdomen for secreting wax; thus he does not forage or build honey or brood comb. He does not have a stinger to defend the hive or himself, yet, found in the abdomen region where the queen and worker bee's stinger is located, one will find the drone's endophallus; his penis. Thus, it is the drone's genitalia that will fundamentally enable him to achieve his life's purpose ~ to mate with a virgin queen bee. It is important to note that all the members, when they sense their hive's temperature is deviating from its proper limit, will either generate heat by shivering, or exhaust heat by moving air (a process called fanning) with their wings, and drones will also participate in this task with the workers.

Nine to twelve days after he emerges from his brood cell, he will be ready to copulate (Couvillon et al., 2010). Generally due to the existence of a limited number of young queens, only a few drones will have the chance to realize their full potential and pass on their semen during a queen bee's virginal flight. Those drones that do mate will die thereafter. If a drone is unsuccessful in mating, as the season moves toward the end of the summer the drone will be ejected from the hive by the worker bees, and eventually die of cold and or starvation (Couvillon et al., 2010). In regions of the world that have severe winters, all drones are driven out of the hive in the autumn. A colony begins to rear drones in spring and their population reaches its peak in late spring and early summer during the swarm season.

Time To Go ☞

The Mating Flight: *Not For the Weak of Heart*

Now that you have been introduced to the cast of characters and their unique roles within the hive, you might find it interesting to learn that the emergence of a mating flight will begin with the worker bees, and if the truth be known, the queen isn't the only member ruling the hive, because the workers have considerable decision making capacity. Thus, three significant concerns unfold in hive that will signal to the workers the need to nurture new queen cells, and they are: colony swarming, supersedure, and queenlessness.

The queen bee's development begins when the worker bees begin building a brood cell fit for a queen; a queen cup. As mentioned earlier they are much larger, constructed vertically, and in addition to the physical cell's structure when a fertilized egg is laid, they are fed only royal jelly until capped. On day 16 when the new queen emerges from her brood cell, she will signal her arrival by making a *piping* noise very familiar to attentive beekeepers which sound like musical note G-Sharp (Seeley, 2010). However, once the queen emerges, as many have witnessed and recorded for hundreds of years, her first deed it to defend her place in the hive. For instance in 1860, Langstroth wrote, "It is the instinctive enmity of young queens to each other, that I have seen one of them, immediately on its emergence from the cell, rush to those of its sisters, and tear to pieces even the imperfect larva… But from these facts, we must now admire her precautions in exposing certain individuals to a mortal hazard" (pgs. 46-47).

After the virgin queen hatches, between the 6-16th day she will be strong enough to fly. On the first sunny afternoon when the temperature is around 15 degrees celsius (60 degrees Fahrenheit); or above, the workers will escort her out the door and she will leave the hive and mate (Root & Root, 1980). It is during this one and only virginal flight that she must secure her place within the hive by collecting enough sperm to use for the rest of her life. To succeed she must mate with as many as 10-12 drones.

During her flight as she enters the mating zone of a cloud of drones, a dozen or perhaps as many as a thousand drones will fly after the queen as she flies in a zigzag manner so that only the strongest airborne drones can overtake her (Smith, 1949). If the queen is unable to make or complete her nuptial flight, for instance should be killed due to weather, the rest of the hive is in peril. However as mentioned earlier, to safeguard the colony and the continuation of a healthy flourishing hive, worker bees would have ensured additional queen cells were developed and protected. Yet, the honeymoon of the bee is short for no sooner does the queen become a bride than she is a widow, and no sooner does the drone become a groom than he passes away (Smith, 1949). But why *might you ask*?

In preparation for his mating mission, the drone's endophallus (penis) will emerge, and this only occurs when he is preparing to copulate. His penis is specially designed to disperse an impressively large amount of semen with tremendous speed and force. Once he's gripped the queen, he inserts his endophallus into the queen (Czekońska & Chuda-Mickiewicz, 2015). At that moment the drone becomes paralyzed and does a back flip and ejaculates semen (Witherell, 1965). Yes this is true, you can't make this stuff up, plus didn't the text begin by stating bees really are amazing? Regrettably drones do not survive copulation because the force that is required causes his internal organs to explode and his penis will be left behind in the queen (Rueppell et., al, 2007; Witherell, 1965). Other drones involved in the mating flight (remember it can be as many as 10), will remove the previous penis, and continue to mate with the queen. When she returns to the hive after her flight the worker bees will take out the last endophallus should one need removal. The queen will store up to 100 million sperm within her oviducts (Winstead, 1989). However, only five to six million are stored within the queen's **spermatheca**. If a queen runs out of sperm in her lifetime, a new generation of queens will mate and produce their own colony. This inevitable situation leads to our final topic of this chapter Queenlessness, Supersedure, and Colony Swarming.

Queenlessness ~ *An Emergency*

When a honey bee queen suddenly dies the hive becomes a melancholy community, but without intervention the colony will be in peril, therefore an urgent and unplanned supersedure occurs. Workers identify several larvae within the proper age range and begin to condition these larvae to become queens (Seeley, 1996; Tew, 2015). Recall the singular difference between a worker and a queen is in the nourishment received during their egg and larva cycle. The workers will therefore feed and nurture prospective queens only royal jelly.

Supersedure

Supersedure is the term often used by beekeepers to describe the replacement of an old queen by her daughters (Blackiston, 2015; Seeley, 1996; Tew, 2015). Apart from the death of a queen, natural supersedure usually occurs at the end of the summer or early autumn, apparently when the colony thinks there is a danger of the old queen not being able to lay fertile eggs. The **fecundity** of the queen bee ordinarily diminishes as she ages. Since the content of her spermathecal has become exhausted, she ceases to lay worker-eggs, thus only drones develop. Moreover, the eggs she does lay are fewer in number and in a less organized pattern. Consequently, when the queen begins to falter, workers will induce her replacement, or supersedure.

Supersedure cells are usually started at roughly the same time so they will emerge within a short time of each other. During supersedure episodes, colonies will occasionally tolerate more than one functional queen in the brood. This is usually because the colony's old queens are is in transition and the situation will likely correct itself (Blackiston, 2015; Tew, 2015). Eventually one queen will become the hive's monarchy. The aging queen will be killed after the supersedure process.

Colony Swarming

Swarming, naturally or intentionally occurs when there is an abundance of nectar and pollen coming in from the fields and the colony is built up to good strength with plenty of brood in all stages in the hive. The hive becomes crowded, thus, the bees may decide to swarm (Smith, 1949; Winston, 1987). The first step in preparing to swarm is the building of queen cells, and then a new home must be found.

Photo Image 2.4: Colony Swarming
Credit: Bildagentur Zoonar GmbH /Shutterstock

In a remarkable example of collective decision-making, swarms of honey bees will choose one of many nest sites that have been located by their scouts (worker bees). Scouts will return and share with their hive what they believed to be a suitable new home. They will communicate the direction and place through a remarkable form of communication known as the Waggle Dance. This dance and how it was discovered will be explored in Chapter 4: Flower Power. Hopefully this has sparked your curiosity. But before we get our groove on, in our next chapter an in-depth examination of the honey bee anatomy will unfold.

Although European honeybees are semi-domesticated, feral honey bees still exist. For instance, they can be found in cracks, rock outcroppings, trees cavities, and attics. And if some bee swarming bees do not have a nuc provided by a beekeeper, or can't find a suitable cavity, they may build a free-hanging nest high up in a tree (See Photo Image 2.5: Wild Beehive in an Apple Tree).

Photo Image 2.5: Wild Honey Beehive in an Apple Tree
⬣ Notice the bee space!
Credit: brandtbolding/Thinkstock

CHAPTER REVIEW QUESTIONS

1. Which describes the developmental stages of the honey bee?
    a. Egg; Larva; Pupa; Adult
    b. Egg; Pupa; Larva; Adult
    c. Pupa; Egg; Pupa; Adult
    d. Larva; Egg; Pupa; Adult

2. Who does NOT have a stinger?
    a. Queen
    b. Female Worker Bee
    c. Drone Bee
    d. Male worker bee

3. Which develops from an unfertilized egg?
    a. Queen
    b. Worker Bee
    c. Drone Bee
    d. None of them; they are all fertilized

4. Beekeepers often use the term 'piping.' What is it?
    a. Cell construction of a failing bee colony
    b. A sound made by an emerging queen
    c. A hive stand made to resemble a pipe form
    d. Fabric used by beekeepers to wrap the hive in cold weather

5. All honey bees can sting.
    a. True
    b. False

6. Which of the following describes the Larva?
    a. Stage at which eyes, legs, and wings grow
    b. Is fed by worker bees
    c. Is about the size of the a piece of rice
    d. Chews its way out of the cell

7. What is the sticky, milky fluid produced by worker bees called?
    a. Bee bread
    b. Royal jelly
    c. Queen brew
    d. Bee milk

8. If the hive is congested and honey and brood cells are plentiful, what might occur?
    a. Honey foraging will increase
    b. The old queen will be superseded
    c. Honey bees will start removing drone larva from cells
    d. Reduction of queen pheromone distribution

9. A queen cells looks like?
    a. A small mushroom
    b. A peanut shell
    c. A banana
    d. A sewing thimble

10. Colonies with young queens are least apt to swarm.
    a. True
    b. False

ACTIVITY

To enhance your understanding and nurture your curiosities check out the following:

I. Google the following to hear the piping sound emitted by the virgin queen as she emerges from her cell. G-sharp: https://www.youtube.com/watch?v=jI7ZludT5I8

II.   Reflection Questions ~ thoughts to ponder once you have completed this chapter
- What is the difference between the food fed to a queen larva and the food fed to a worker or drone larva?
- Why would it be important for a beekeeper to know how to identify their brood cells?

KEY TERMS

Bee Bread
- Food made from honey and pollen that is feed to the open brood; worker and drone larvae

Brood
- Term used to describe the eggs, larva and pupa in the honey bee hive

Comb
- A back-to-back collection of hexagonal cells that are made of beeswax and used by bees to store food and raise brood.

Cuticle
- Covers the body of bee, which forms an exoskeleton (external skeleton). The cuticle protects the internal organs and prevents water loss

Eusocial
- Live cooperatively in multigenerational groups to aid a few reproductive members. These species often exhibit task specialization, which makes them efficient in gathering resources
- Eusocial insects, for example, are true social species that possess three characteristics: cooperative brood care, overlap of two or more generations with offspring assisting with brood care, and reproductive division of labor. In a broad sense, the term "social" is often used for pre- and subsocial insects that have fewer than three of the characteristics of eusociality

Fecundity
- The ability to produce an abundance of offspring or new growth; fertility

Propolis
- A sticky substance collected from plants used to plug holes and stick things together in the hive; *Bee glue*

Supersedure
- The replacement of an old or inferior queen bee by a young or superior queen. The act or process of superseding

Chapter 2: Review and Study Notes

Chapter 2: Review and Study Notes

Chapter 3
The Anatomy of the Honey Bee

"Such bees! Bilbo had never seen anything like them.
"If one were to sting me," He thought "I should swell up as big as I am!"

~ J.R.R. Tolkien, *The Hobbit* ~

CHAPTER OBJECTIVES

After reading this chapter you should be able to:

1. Distinguish and describe the bee's three distinct parts; Head, Thorax and Abdomen
2. Identify and explain the internal and external structures of the honey bee
3. Draw and label the honey bee anatomy
4. Describe the functions of the bee's anatomy and how it contributes to the bee's tasks

Introduction:
European Honey Bee: *Apis mellifera*

The European honey bee is one of our most productive earthly creatures. Their complex body parts provide them the capability to perform a broad range of athletic, acrobatic and specific tasks (See Photo Image 3.1: The Exterior of the Honey Bee). In Chapter 2 the honey bee colony described how the three members collectively contribute to the overall survival and well-being of the hive. Recall, only the worker bees participate in brood rearing, comb building (wax) and foraging. Whereas drones and queens have unique specializations associated with reproduction. As such different honey bee anatomy exits. The following chapter will explore the important structures on and inside the bee.

The Honey Bee's Skeleton

As a member of the insect class (insecta), all honey bees share similar characteristics with other insects. The honey bee is covered with a thick layer of **cuticle**, that entomologists call an exoskeleton (Ellis, 2015). This skeleton is on the bee's exterior, it's rigid, and covered with layers of wax. The **exoskeleton's** main component is **chitin**, which is a polymer of glucose that can support a lot of weight with very little material. This external skeleton also protects bees from losing water (desiccation) and it provides them protection from predators. An additional advantage of this chitin-containing exoskeleton is that it prevents bees from growing continually; instead, they must shed their skin periodically during the larva stage, but will remain the same size until it emerges in its adult form (Blackiston, 2015).

Photo Image 3.1: The Exterior of the Honey Bee
⬡ Observe the three distinct parts; the head, thorax and abdomen. The wings, eyes, antennae, branch hair are also discernable. Note three of its 6 legs, the claws and a packed pollen sac
Credit: Billion Photos/Shutterstock

Nearly the entire bee is covered with soft fuzzy hair, yet unlike human hair that consists of a single shaft, under the microscope a bee's hair appears to be branched (See Illustration 3.1: Honey Bee Wings, Antennae, Branched Hair).

They could in appearance be compared to the needles on a spruce tree, or a pipe cleaner; an art supply you might have used in childhood (Winston, 1987). These hairs are vital as they allow bees to feel. As they forage, these hairs will build up an electrostatic charge causing pollen to jump onto the bee's body as she visits flowers, and this behaviour generates pollination (Blackiston, 2015; Ellis, 2015). Later, when she returns to the hive the pollen will be combed off by fellow bees and used to make beebread.

The bee's exoskeleton and internal structures are arranged in three distinct parts; head, thorax and abdomen, each of which has a number of **segments** and specialized parts and functions. This chapter will examine the internal and external structures the honey bee and it will commence with the head (See Photo Image 3.1: The Exterior of the Honey Bee).

The Head

Almost everything that a honey bee uses to sense the outside world is part of or connected to the head, as it is the center of information gathering (Ellis, 2015). When viewed under a microscope one might consider the head to be an alarming menacing sight with its enormous eyes and giant jaw (See Photo Image 3.2). The head however, is highly specialized and rather harmless. Its glands produce various chemical **pheromones** used for communication, and the production of the all-important royal jelly; the secreted substance used to feed the brood. Consuming, feeding and sharing food are essential tasks that are possible due to the head's anatomy (Tew, 2015; Warton et. al., 2007; Winston, 1987).

Physically, the honey bee's head is flat and somewhat triangular in shape. The organs on or inside the head are: the antennae, eyes, mouth parts, and its internal structures. Let's take a closer look at these parts (See Photo Image 3.1).

The Eyes

The honey bee's visual perception is possible due to their two different types of eyes; compound and ocelli eyes. Their two compound eyes cover a large part of the head's surface, and are composed of thousands of ommatidia, or light –sensitive cells (See Photo Images: 3.1 and 3.2). These cells are used to distinguish light, see colour, patterns, and movement to read the direction from the sun's ultraviolent rays (Wilson-Rich, 2014). The honey bee's visual world is quite unique in that they see primarily blues and greens, and some other colours, but curiously bees see what humans cannot; ultraviolent. "Through our eyes the world looks more yellow and red, while the bee sees it as far more blue and purple, and bees cannot see the red end of the spectrum" (Wilson-Rich, 2014, p. 32). The images from all these lenses are believed to converge into a single image in the bee's brain (Ellis, 2015).

In addition to visual motion perception, the compound eyes can also perceive airflow using sensory hairs. In a study conducted by Nesse in 1965, it was discovered that when these hairs were remove with a miniature scalpel, the workers lost their ability to find their way to accustomed feeding sites under windy conditions, presumably because they could no longer compensate wind speed during flight.

In terms of physical size, the drone has the largest compound eyes to enhance his vision, which supports him during mating (recall this is his essential task). His huge wrap-around compound eyes make the drone easy to identify and distinguish from the queen, whose eyes are slightly smaller than the worker bee (Blackiston, 2015; Warton et. al., 2007; Wilson-Rich, 2014; Winston, 1987).

The second type of eye is called the **ocelli**; also referred to as the three simple eyes. They are located on the top of their head and arranged in a triangle pattern. Each contains only one lens that does not focus or make images, but functions solely to detect light intensity which helps to regulate **diurnal** activity patterns for orientation. This ability is essential considering the poor or diminished visual acuity conditions within the hive (Ellis, 2015). Compared to the compound eyes, the function of ocelli eyes is less understood.

Photo Image 3.2: Close up of a Worker Bee Head
⬡ Notice the antennae, mandibles, branch hair; the ocelli eyes are also discernable
Credit: MURGVI /Shutterstock

Antennae

The honey bee spends a significant part of their life living in the dark since their daily activities include time spent either inside tree hollows if living in nature, or in man-made hives (the Langstroth Hive). Since darkness can produce poor visual acuity (sight) once they enter the hive alternative navigating options are essential, thus, the ability to smell and touch is critical, and their antennae support this process (Briant, 1984).

Every bee has two antennae attached at its forehead; one on each side, which house thousands of sensory organs. Structurally, the bee's antennae are bent and made up of several segments, which are connected with an elbow-like joint. There are three key parts, the pedicel, scape, and the flagellum.

A worker bee has 10 segments and drones have 11 segments on each flagellum. Thus, drone bees have a total of 13 segments and the workers have 12 (See Illustration 3.1: Honey Bee Wings, Antennae, Branched Hair).

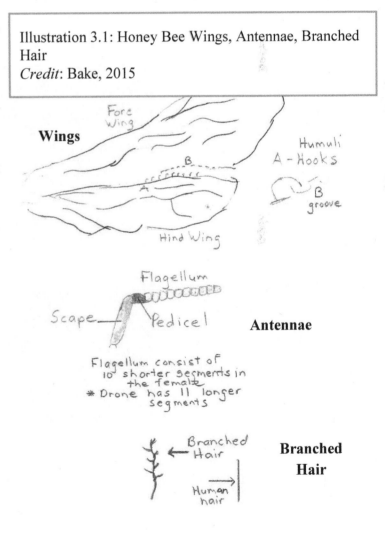

Illustration 3.1: Honey Bee Wings, Antennae, Branched Hair
Credit: Bake, 2015

The antennae are the noses of the honey bee. The role the bee's antennae played in smell was first discovered by Karl von Frisch; his contributions will be examined in Chapter 4. Through his research von Frisch demonstrated that workers could be trained to visit dishes which contained odours of natural flowers or essential oils, but when the bee's antennae were surgically removed, this olfactory discrimination ability was eliminated (von Frisch, 1963).

The antennae's also have branched hairs, which further support the bee's ability to detect and feel. Some branched hairs are specialized for touch (mechanoreceptors), others for taste (gustatory receptors) and some for smell (odour receptors). These hairs are used to identify flowers, water, the colony, and *maybe even you*!

Mouth Parts

The honey bee's mouth structure is combined so they can chew and suck, which allows them to manipulate solid material as well as lap up liquids. This ability distinguishes them from most insects as they can generally only do one of these two functions. For instance grasshoppers can only chew and moths that can only suck (Linghua, 2015). This dual ability is accomplished because they possess two distinct mouth parts; the **proboscis** and **mandibles** (Blackiston, 2015; Ellis, 2015).

Most of us are familiar with those noisemakers that show up at birthday and New Year's Eve parties. You know the ones that unroll when you toot them! The worker honey bees **proboscis** is much like those party favours only without the "toot." When the bee is at rest, this organ is retracted ~ in an unfolded position. When the bee is using it to fulfill its many roles it will be extended. The proboscis is composed of two organs, the maxillae and the labium. The bee can bend them into a tube shape; therefore it enables them to suck up liquids such

Photo Image 3.3: Trophallaxis
- In the hive workers are exchanging food using their proboscis. Can you identify other body parts?
Credit: Zoonar RF /Thinkstock

as, nectar, water, and honey when inside the hive (Langstroth, 1860; Wilson-Rich, 2014). Within the hive the proboscis is used to lick pheromones from the queen and exchanging them with other workers. The proboscis is also essential in the food exchanging process; trophallaxis, which occurs between bees (See Photo Image 3.3: Trophallaxis). Langstroth (1860) specifically described the worker bee's proboscis as "not larger than a very small pea, and so perfectly transparent as to appear, when filled to be the same color with its contents (p. 56). Chapter 4: Flower Power will expand upon the role trophallaxis also has in honey bee communication. Although the worker's proboscis is exceedingly curious to observe, the drone's proboscis is not suitably sized for gathering nectar, thus he does not forage (Langstroth, 1860; Winston, 1987).

The **mandibles** are the honey bee's other mouth parts which are their jaw, and it is connected to their head by powerful muscles that can be opened and closed. However, by human standards they are too small to injure if they were to bite. The mandibles have numerous functions and are essential to survival, as they support the bee's ability to collect and chew pollen, feed larvae, chew wood, soften and manipulate wax when building brood and storage cells, clean other bees, and cling to surfaces, and drag dead bees out of the hive. But to other bees, insects (mites), hive robbers and other creatures that attempt to move into their hive, their bite can be fierce when needed (Linghua, 2015; Stell, 2012).

Head's Internal Organs

The main internal organs in the head are:
- The brain
- The subesophageal ganglion: the main component of the nervous system
- The ventral nerve cord that runs all the way through the thorax to the abdomen

The bee's sophisticated brain receives inputs from the compound eyes which are attached to the optic lobes. The next largest input is from the antennae (antenna lobes). Also significant is the area in the middle of the brain called the mushroom body. As its name would suggest, visually the cross section resembles two mushrooms. It is a prominent and striking structure in the brain of several invertebrates. It has a long stalk crowned with a cap of cell bodies (neurons), also known as Kenyon cells. There are approximately 175,000 neurons per mushroom (Campbell and Turner, 2010; Kenyon, 1896; Fahrbach et. al., 1995; Heisenberg, 1998). Compare this number to the smaller fruit fly's brain which only possesses about 2,500 (Campbell & Turner, 2010). This area is also known to be involved in olfactory learning, and in an insects' short and long term memory formation (Heisenberg, 1998).

Chart 3. 1: Honey Bee Exocrine Glands	
Glandular System: The glands of the worker bees are used for four basic functions; Communication, Defense, Food Processing and Wax Production	

Mandibular glands: A simple sac-like structure attached to each of the mandibles	• **In the queen**:
	• The source of the powerful **queen pheromone**
	  ➢ Suppresses the construction of emergency queen cells
	  ➢ Inhibits ovary development in the worker bees
	  ➢ Attracts the attendant workers (worker bees)
	  ➢ Enables her to identify members of her own colony
	  ➢ Attracts drones during the mating flight
	• **In the drone:**
	  ➢ Assists in the formation of drone gatherings – in drone congregation areas (DCA's) which appear in open fields
	• **In young worker bees:**
	  ➢ Produces a lipid-rich white substance, is mixed with a secretion to make royal jelly
	• **In old worker bees (foragers)**:
	  ➢ Produces heptanone, the alarm pheromone
	• The discovery of these glands in 1846 is attributed to Meckel

Nasonov gland	• Workers release a pheromone to orient returning forager back to the hive • To broadcast this scent, bees raise their abdomens, which contain the glands, and fan their wings vigorously
Hypopharyngeal gland	• Produce larval brood food and protein-rich sections; royal jelly when the worker is a nurse bee • When the worker starts to forage it synthesize enzymes involved in the conversion of sucrose to simple sugars and honey production
Salivary glands	• Produces saliva; mixes with wax scales to change physical property of wax
Koschevnikov gland	• Releases alarm pheromone to attract other bees to attack/sting offender • In the **queen** it is the product responsible for the formation of the clusters of court bees that surround her
Wax glands	• Located in the lower part of the worker's abdomen (4 in total) • The worker begins to secrete wax 12 days after emerging • Six days later, the gland degenerates and the worker stops comb-building
Sources; Dade, 2009; Fahrbach et. al., 1995; Heisenberg; 1998; Kenyon, 1896; Ohasi et al., 1999; Patel et al., 1960; Shell, 2012; Smith, 1949; White et al., 1963; Winston, 1987	

Fun Fact: How did mushroom body research start? In 1850, Felix Dujardin showed that the size of the mushroom body was correlated with the intricacy of social behaviour in different species of bees. Dujardin suggested that mushroom bodies control aspects of insect behaviour that are not just simple reflexes and even speculated that they might play a role in 'free will' (Campbell and Turner, 2010). Check out the link in ACTIVITIES to view this region of the brain.

Within the brain there are endocrine organs attached to the nerve cords, and they are close to the esophagus (the food canal). One is called the corpora allata. This hormone is involved in both the queen-worker differentiation, and the division of labour in workers. The other organ is called the corpora cardiac, which is a neurohemal organ that stores and releases the hormone prothoracicotropic (PTTH). It regulates the bee's developmental timing and body size (McBrayer et. al., 2008). Lastly, the bee has a number of exocrine glands (See Chart 3. 1: Honey Bee Exocrine Glands).

Thorax

The thorax constitutes the middle part of the bee that connects the head to the abdomen, and is the center for locomotion. It has three segments; the Prothorax, Mesothorax and the Metathorax each with a pair of spiracles for letting in air (See Illustration 3.2: Anatomy of the Honey Bee and Photo Image 3.1: The Exterior of the Honey).

Spiracles

Spiracles are tiny holes and the means by which a bee breathes. This is why it is dangerous to spray water on bees in your garden, or why you will observe them rushing back to the hive when it rains. Water can cause them to drown. Spiracles are located along the sides of a bee's thorax and abdomen. There are 10 spiracles on each side, a total of 20. Six are located on the thorax, and the other 14 are located on the abdomen (Shell, 2012). The abdomen spiracles are all similar, but those of the thorax are not. The first spiracles are hidden beneath the spiracle lobe, which is a large hair-fringed backward extension located on the first thoracic segment. The bee's trachea (breathing tubes) is attached to these spiracles. (See Illustration 3.2: Anatomy of the Honey Bee). It is through the first hole in the thorax that tracheal mites gain access to the bee's trachea (See Chapter 6, Chart 6.1: Overview of Honey Bee Diseases and Pests). The second spiracle lies below the wings, halfway between the fore-wing and hind-wing. The third spiracle is the largest, and they are easily seen on each side of the bee's thorax (Shell, 2012).

A spiracle is an important part of the bees open circulatory system. An open circulatory system indicates that bees do not have veins or arteries, but rather all their internal organ are bathed in a liquid called 'hemolymph' (a mix of blood and lymphatic fluid). Bees breathe through this complex network structure of tracheas and air sacs (Shell, 2012). Oxygen is vacuumed into the body through the spiracles on each segment by the expansion of the air sacs. The spiracles are then closed and the air sacs are compressed to force the air into smaller tracheas, which become smaller and smaller until individual tubules reach individual cells.

Illustration 3.2: Anatomy of the Honey Bee
Credit: Bake, 2015

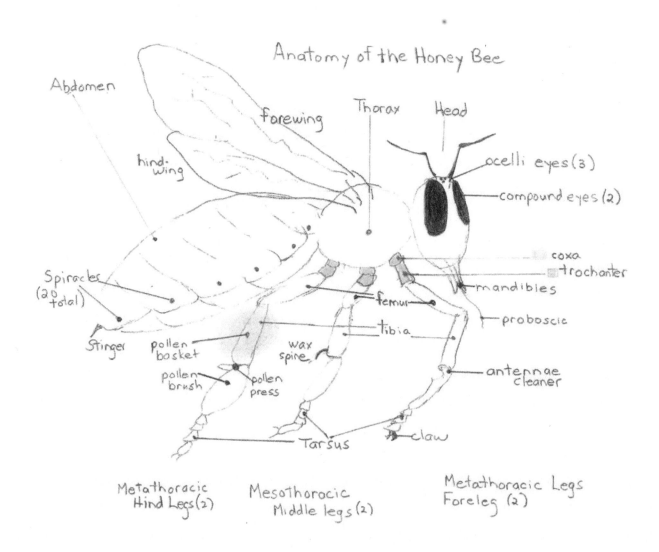

Anatomy of the Honey Bee

Wings

How many wings does a honey bee have? The answer is four. The front pair is the largest, and are attached to the Mesothorax, whereas the hindwings are smaller and attached to the Metathorax. To ensure an effective synchronized flight the wings become hooked together once the bee is airborne. This is accomplished by a row of wing hooks called humuli, (singular: humulus) that are located on the hind wings that will hitch into a fold on the rear edge of the front wings (See Illustration 3.1: Honey Bee Wings, Antennae, Branched Hair). The wings are powered by two sets of muscles inside the thorax, the longitudinal and vertical muscles; and endurance is critical.

Photo Image 3.4: Honey Bee in Flight
● Notice the wings. What other parts of the honey bees' anatomy can you identify?
Credit: De tobkatrina /Shutterstock

According to British Beekeepers Association, it is possible for bees to fly as far as 5 miles for food; however an average distance would be less than a mile from the hive. (See Photo Image 3.4: Honey Bee in Flight).

Fun Fact: A strong colony flies the equivalent distance of the earth to the moon every day. The normal top speed of a worker would be about 21-28 km/h (15-20 mph), when flying to a food source, and it is reduced to about 17 km/h (12 mph), when returning since she will be weighed down with nectar, pollen, propolis or water (British Beekeepers Association).

The honey bee's wing size is one part of the bee's anatomy that differs between the caste (Bujok et al., 2002; Winston, 1987). For instance, the worker bee has the smallest wings and the queen the largest. The bee's wings are also part of their heating system. Due to the varied range of habitats and environments in which bees exist, they have evolved their ability to heat their wings up to 30 degrees Celsius (86 Fahrenheit) on a cold winter morning, and without moving them (Bujok et al., 2002).

Legs

Bees have three pairs of legs, all attached to the thorax with one pair located on each thoracic segment. Their primary function is to help the bee walk and run, but specialized parts serve specific purposes. The legs are very adaptable, with claws on the last tarsomere, allowing bees to securely grip rough surfaces (tree trunks). Conversely they also have a soft pad (arolium) to allow them to walk on smooth surfaces, for instance grass and leaves (See Illustration 3.2: Anatomy of the Honey Bee).

Photo Image 3.5: Bees Bridge Swarm
- If a natural swarm takes place the need to locate a new hive is critical
- The bridge is a living chain formed by the bees when they uncover an environment in nature that might be a suitable location to establish a new hive. Once situated, and meeting the necessary hive requirements, they will hold onto each other's middle legs, as they use their front legs to grab the steady flow of wax that is being secreted from their abdominal glands. This wax will provide the necessary hive (comb) making material.
- Cell upon cell and row upon row the honey comb (hive) is made. The more cells that can be made, the more eggs that can be laid and bees born, thus the new colony's chance at survival is enhanced.

Credit: Viesinsh/Thinkstock

The bee's three pairs of legs have the same basic structure. They all have six segments that can be flexed at any of the six joint. This provides them that acrobatic flexibility necessary to achieve so many of their various tasks (See Photo Image 3.5: Bees Bridge Swarm). At the tip of each leg is the pretarsus, which includes the tarsal claws and suction creating pads. Not only are these tips taste receptors, but the claws and suction creating pads facilitates the bee's ability to cling to surfaces, move horizontally and vertically when in the hive or in nature, as well as hang on to other bees when swarming. The tarsals also assist in manipulating wax and building comb. Yet, differences do exist. For instance, each pair differs in size and shape, and each one has a different 'tool' designed for different functions (Bujok et al., 2002; Winston, 1987). Let's explore these six legs in more detail, See Illustration 3.2: Anatomy of the Honey Bee).

Front legs (*Pro*thoracic Legs)

The two front legs are used for sweeping pollen and other particles from the head, eyes and mouth parts. The front leg also has a small groove that acts as an antenna comb (cleaner) to remove pollen from the bee's antenna to ensure the bee's sensory functions are not impaired (Dade, 2009; Seeley, 2010).

The Middle legs (*Meso*thoracic Legs)

The **middle legs** are used by the worker bee to brush, pack, and load pollen onto the pollen baskets that are part of the hind legs, and then carry the pollen and propolis back to the hive. **Propolis** is the sticky resinous substance that the bees collect (See Illustration 3.2: Anatomy of the Honey Bee).

Photo Image 3.6: Honey Bee Foraging
⬡ Notice how she is using her legs to clasp onto the stem
Credit: GlobalPMore / Thinkstock

The Hind legs (Metathoracic Legs)

The hind legs are specialized on the worker. It is here where you will quickly notice the pollen basket (corbicula), located on the tibia of the hind legs. Upon close examination you will also notice that the pollen basket is a smooth, concave area of the outer hind leg (See Photo Image 3.6: Honey Bee foraging). The hind leg also contains a pollen press and special comb used for packing pollen when preparing to return to the hive. This surface also has hairs on the edges and a central long bristle that extends through the pollen pellet or propolis to ensure the foragers (worker bees) are successfully able to transport pollen and propolis. During a warm sunny day in the garden you might catch of glimpse of a bright yellow ball attached to a busy bee's hind legs (Dade, 2009; Seeley, 2010).

The Abdomen

The abdomen of all three honey bee types is generally hairy. In queens and workers there are 10 segments in total but only seven abdominal segments are visible. On the other hand the drone bee has only nine segments, and eight are visible. Each segment has yellow and black bands on them, and the older the bee the greater proportion of black bands than yellow. Otherwise the abdominal has no other external structure of interest. Each segment has two plates, which are the **tergite (**is the dorsal portion; backside) and **the sternite plates** (underneath).

Photo Image 3.7: Queen and Workers
⬡ Notice the difference in physical size but also the wings of the workers to the queen
Credit: Inventori/Thinkstock

The tergites overlap one another and are joined together with an intersegmental membrane that provides the bee a great degree of flexibility. The tergites also overlap with the sternites (the underside;

bottom of the abdomen), and they too are joined with a flexible membrane. These elastic membranes are essential because they allow the abdomen the ability to expand and contract which is vital to the bee's survival. For instance, they permit the bee to pump air in and out of the air sacs, eliminate its waste, and expand when the stomach becomes engorged with nectar or water (Dade, 2009; Seeley, 2010). This expansion also guarantees her ability to consume a large quantity of honey which is crucial fuel when preparing to leave the hive to forage.

The abdomen is also the region where you will locate the wax secretion glands. When wax is produced the bee will grab it with its font legs, and move it up towards its mouth, manipulate it with its mandibles and turn it into comb. The abdomen muscles of the drone are much stronger than the worker to ensure he has the strength necessary to successfully fulfil the mating ritual.

Internally the abdomen contains most of the organs systems and glands. Included are its digestive organs, reproductive organs, wax and scent glands (workers only), and the worker and queen bee's infamous stinger (ovipositor), which are held inside a chamber at the tip of the abdomen. The stinger has two components, the poison gland (filled with colourless liquid when fresh) and the alkaline gland (which may appear yellow). Also contained internally at the tip of the drone's abdomen is his endophallus; his reproductive organ (Dade, 2009).

Wax Scales

When worker are about 6-12 days old they can begin producing wax scales in their two pairs of wax glands which are located on the 4th and 7th abdominal segments. All developing workers need to eat pollen during their 5th and 6th day of life in order to produce wax thereafter. The glands are concealed from view, but the wax scales they produce can be seen, and ordinarily with the naked eye. As the workers chew and mix the wax with their saliva, their previous thin and quite clear appearance turns whitish in colour (Dade, 2009; Seeley, 2010).

Digestive and Excretory Systems

Honey Stomach (Crop)

The honey stomach (Crop) is connected to the mouth via the long esophagus. In fact the honey stomach is part of the esophagus that expands when the honey bee swallows nectar. Imagine the honey stomach as an expandable bag; a balloon. It holds the honey which is the fuel source needed when foraging, and stores the collected water and nectar (Dade, 2009; Seeley, 2010). After foraging when the honey stomach is full, the bee returns to transfer their contents to a waiting worker in a process called **trophallaxis** (See Photo Image 3.3: Trophallaxis). Once the honey is passed to an inside (house) worker bee, the process of converting nectar into honey begins (See Illustration 3.3: Internal Organs of the Honey Bee).

Excretion

Honey bees do not defecate in their hives. Thus, their rectums expand considerably to hold waste material stored during the winter, while they wait for the warm flying weather in the spring to eliminate their accumulated feces.

Queen's Reproductive System

The queen's two ovaries are huge to facilitate her egg-laying function. Each ovary contains 150-180 egg producing **ovarioles**, compared to the worker ovaries which are much smaller and have only 2-12 ovarioles. The Queen's ovarioles can produce an unlimited number of eggs; up to one million or more during her lifetime. When an egg is released it travels down an oviduct past the **spermathecal,** which is a circular sack. Before the queen's mating flight the spermatheca is filled with spermathecal fluid. Between the 6-16th day after the virgin queen hatches, she will take her mating flight. The spermatheca will hold the sperm the queen amasses while mating. After mating the spermatheca is filled with **spermatozoa** (Warton et. al., 2007; Dallai, 1975; Snodgrass, 1956). The spermatheca can hold around 7 million sperm, and it generally takes 2-4 years before all the sperm are used. Each time she lays an egg she will release only a few sperm. She must use her sperm judiciously, because once she runs out, as you might recall from Chapter 2, she will be **superseded** by her colony (Harbo, 1979; Velthuis, 1970). On might state that it is therefore the amount of sperm the queen has that determines her lifespan.

Drone's Reproductive Organs

Having studied the mating flight of the honey bee, this ritual now clarifies why the various anatomical differences exist between the bees. In a honey bee colony drones are responsible for producing semen and transmitting it to the queen during copulation (Czekońska & Chuda-Mickiewicz, 2015).The drone endophallus; penis, will only emerge when mating, and just before this occurs he will use his pair of copulatory claspers to grip the queen. This is essential since a drone must penetrate the queen mid-flight. Once he has mounted her he inserts his endophallus, which is designed to disperse an impressively large amount of semen with tremendous speed and force. This process will rip open the male's abdomen, and cause his death (Boes, 2010; Czekońska & Chuda-Mickiewicz, 2015).

Illustration 3.3: Internal Organs of the Honey Bee
Credit: Bake, 2015

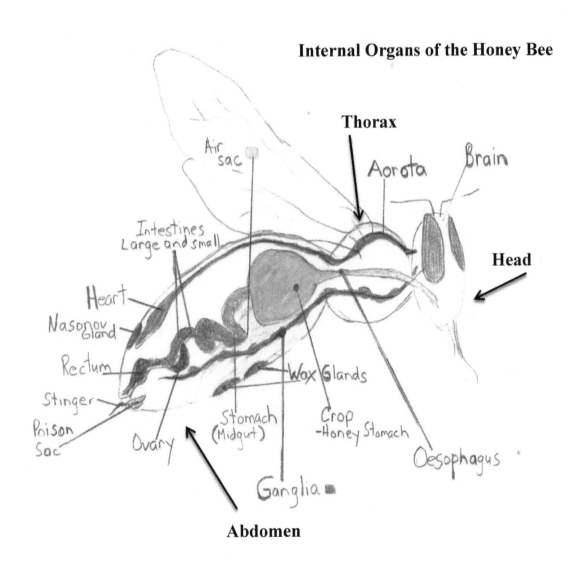

Internal Organs of the Honey Bee

Stinger

The drone does not have a stinger; therefore he cannot defend himself or the hive. On the other hand the queen stinger will be used when battling against rival queens. Her stinger's barbs are small so the stinger can be retracted after being used. It is a very different reality unfortunately for the worker bee. The workers stinger has large barbs preventing it from being pulled out after it stings, and the result for her is death. An interesting point to note is that when she does sting an alarm pheromone is released (Koschevnikov gland) that "identifies" her target; the victim, thus sending a signal to other bees to attack and sting. This alarm pheromone is but one of the many ways in which the honey bees communicates, and this complex and fascinating system will be explored in Chapter 4: Flower Power.

CHAPTER REVIEW QUESTIONS

1. Which statement describes the size of the honey bee's compound eyes?
    a. The Worker has the largest
    b. The Queen has the largest
    c. The Drone has the largest
    d. They all have the same size compound eyes

2. What term describes a component of the bee's proboscis?
    a. The spiracles
    b. The chitin
    c. The trophallaxis
    d. The labium

3. Which part of the honey bee anatomy allows it to breath?
    a. The trophallaxis
    b. The spiracles
    c. The ocellies
    d. The chitin

4. How many eyes and spiracles are found on a bee's body?
    a. 5 eyes; 18 spiracles
    b. 5 eyes; 20 spiracles
    c. 6 eyes; 18 spiracles
    d. 6 eyes; 20 spiracles

5. Exocrine glands inside the honey bee head produce powerful pheromones.
    a. True
    b. False

6. While blowing one of these on New Year's Eve, what honey bee part might you recall?
   a. The proboscis
   b. The spiracles
   c. The ocellies
   d. The trophallaxis

7. Before mating, what does the male bee extend?
   a. Proboscis
   b. Stinger
   c. Endophallus
   d. Mandibles

8. Which statement does NOT accurately describe the honey bee anatomy?
   a. Thorax is where you will find all the bee's wings
   b. Abdomen is where you will find the stinger in all bees
   c. Abdomen is where you will locate some but not all the spiracles
   d. Head is where you will locate all the honey bee eyes

9. Which part of the honey bee anatomy has been referred to as the "mushroom body"?
   a. The chitin
   b. The brain
   c. The trophallaxis
   d. The spiracles

10. What is the main component of the bee's exoskeleton?
    a. The spiracles
    b. The ocellies
    c. The chitin
    d. The trophallaxis

ACTIVITY

To enhance your understanding and nurture your curiosities check out the following:

I. Online; test your bee anatomy knowledge
    - http://www.purposegames.com/game/anatomy-of-a-honey-bee-game

II. Mushroom body of the Honey bee brain
    - https://www.youtube.com/watch?v=wBGkS9a1kBE

III. Overview of the honey bee's anatomy
    - http://www.understandingbeeanatomy.com/tag/honeybee/

KEY TERMS

Chitin
- The honey bees exoskeleton's main component
- Is a polymer of glucose that can support a lot of weight with very little material

Cuticle
- It is on the outside, rigid, and covered with layers of wax.

Diurnality
- Is a form of animal behaviour characterized by activity during the day, with a period of sleeping, or other inactivity, at night

Gustatory: gus·ta·to·ry
- Concerned with tasting (eating), or the sense of taste

Humuli
- A small hook or hooklike projection, especially one of a number linking the fore - and hind wings of a bee or wasp

Kenyon cells
- Named after Frederick Kenyon who first applied the Golgi staining technique to the insect brain

Mandibles
- Pair of appendages near the insect's mouth, and their function is typically to grasp, crush, or cut the insect's food, or to defend against predators or rivals

Pheromones: pher·o·mone (ferə͵mōn)
- A chemical substance produced and released into the environment by an animal, especially a mammal or an insect, affecting the behaviour or physiology of others of its species

Proboscis: (prəˈbäskis)
- An elongated sucking mouthpart that is typically tubular and flexible

Segment
- Each of the parts into which something is or may be divided

Tergum (plural *terga*)
- Latin for "the back"
- Is the dorsal portion (backside)

Chapter 3: Review and Study Notes

Chapter 3: Review and Study Notes

Chapter 4: Flower Power

"The richness I achieve comes from nature, the source of my inspiration."

~ Claude Monet (1840-1926) ~

CHAPTER OBJECTIVES

After reading this chapter you should be able to:

1. Explain how Karl von Frisch advanced our honey bee knowledge
2. Describe foraging behaviour and the waggle dance
3. Understand the use of Latin Names for plants
4. Draw and record basic plant anatomy
5. Explain pollination and fertilization
6. Compare and contrast pollen and nectar

Introduction

This chapter will focus on two main subjects. It will expand upon Chapters Two and Three, and examine honey bee communication. Karl von Frisch will be introduced to show how his research advanced our understanding of the honey bee and its survival. This chapter will also provide an introduction to basic plant anatomy, pollen, pollination and fertilization. By no means will this content provide a complete and exhaustive examination of any of these specialized areas of scholarship and research. What this information will do is provide important insights and deepen your understanding of how various themes connect to the environment, the honey bee and our economy. Moreover, these topics may even solidify, or, inspire you to pursue a new career path.

Foraging and Communication

Honey bees are the only creatures apart from us human who communicate by dancing. They dance in spring, summer and autumn, in the dark of the hive, on selected parts of the comb (Zablotny, 2009). This important social behaviour empowers them to quickly mobilize a great number of foragers to gather food resources that may only be available for a short period of time, because nectar secretion is time sensitive. It depends on the warmth of the sun and the direction of the wind and the earth's moisture. Each flower blossom has its own preference as to when these conditions are right. Their capacity to make judgements and precisely communicate food and water location is not only critical to their survival, but it is one of the bee's most interesting behaviours.

Wilson (2014), likened the bees decision making process with humans when he wrote, "We've seen numerous parallels between how bees work and make decisions and corresponding human strategies that are suited to contemporary human societies" (p. 195). For instance, when living in groups, there's wisdom in finding a way for members to make better decisions collectivity than as individuals. Thus, planning is delivered through an open and fair competition of ideas based on a collection of information that is shared across a many individuals; instead of a select few. This leads to the next question, how and when did the bee's ability to collectively communicate and problem solve first become known to the human species? It's time to meet Karl von Frisch.

Karl von Frisch

Karl von Frisch was born in 1886, and died in 1982 at the age of 96. He was an Austrian **ethologist**, and he focused his work on investigating the honey bees' sensory perception (See Photo Image 4.1: Portrait of Karl von Frisch). **Sensory physiology** is the study of seeing, hearing, feeling, smelling, tasting, and the sense of balance, and the way in which biological mechanisms convert physical events (American Psychological Association, 2002). **Ethology** is the scientific and objective study of animal behaviour, with an emphasis on behaviour under natural conditions, and viewing behaviour as an evolutionarily adaptive trait. Many naturalists have studied aspects of animal behaviour throughout history, but it began with well-known and celebrated ethologist Charles Darwin (See Photo Image 4.4: Charles Darwin).

Photo Image 4.1: Portrait of Karl von Frisch, ca 1920.
Credit: Photographer unknown/ Public domain via Wikimedia Commons

After devoting five decades (50 years) of his to life studying the honey bee's communication process, in 1967, Karl von Frisch authored, *The Dance Language and Orientation of Bees.* Later in 1973, Von Frisch was awarded the Nobel Prize in Physiology or Medicine for his landmark research on the waggle dance language. The Nobel Prize in Physiology or Medicine is awarded once a year for outstanding discoveries in the fields of life sciences and medicine. Von Frisch's award bestowed public recognition that non-human animals possess a symbolic means of communication (The Nobel Prize.Org).

Karl von Frisch's decades of bee research however were not conducted in the safety of an apiary. Some of his most important work was accomplished during the often life-threatening circumstances of WWII and the German Reich. During the mid-1930s until the end of WW2, Germany had passed their *Civil Service Law* of 1937, which required all public servants to provide proof of **Aryan** ancestry. When it was discovered that von Frisch's maternal grandmother was Jewish he lost his privileges to teach at the University of Munich. Yet, in Tania Munz's book (2016), *The Dancing Bees Karl von Frisch and the Discovery of the Honeybee Language*, Munz goes one step further to state that von Frisch was triply vulnerable, not only because of his grandmother, but because his laboratory employed many Jewish researchers, and, he had enemies driven by either professional jealousy or their anti-Semitism beliefs. While additional motions were underway to forbid him from working altogether because of his Jewish ancestry, influential friends managed to intervene on his behalf, and government officials allowed him to continue his research. While much of Europe lay buried under the wreckage of World War Two, the bee population throughout Europe was also facing hazardous effects caused by a bee plague. Since the German government understood the significant role pollinating insects played in crop production, the Ministry of Food and Agriculture deemed von Frisch's research critical to the Reich's food supply. Years later, Karl von Frisch would state that the bees saved his life.

After WW2 ended, in 1946, von Frisch penned a letter from his home in Austria to a fellow animal behaviourist to report his sensational findings about the language of bees. He celebrated his research, which illuminated the finding that workers, when returning from foraging do in fact communicate to their colony the distance and direction of a food source by means of "dances". Yes, that's correct; they communicate, and share information with each other regarding the location and quantity of food resources, and we have Karl von Frisch to thank for those original academic insights.

The Waggle Dance
Are You Ready to Bee Bop ~ Or is it "Hive Talking"?

Credit: dedalukas/Thinkstock

Would you be surprised to learn that your favourite pint of honey required roughly 5 million honey bee flower visits (Blackiston, 2015)? So it begs the question, how is this accomplished? It's what bees do each day, when the honey bee scouts leave their colony and scatter several miles in various directions searching for potential bounties. Workers generally forage a radius of four-to-five kilomters (two-to-three mile) from the hive in search of food. That is the equivalent of over 8,000 acres (Blackiston, 2015). But besides the gift of honey that might await us humans, their foraging is extremely personal because water, nectar, pollen, and propolis (resin collected from trees) are crucial to the colony's well-being and survival. Nectar is not only an important source for making honey, it also provides sugar that is the primary source of energy for the bees' wing muscles that will not only be used for flying, but to heat the hive during the winter season.

Pollen, another foraging reward, provides the protein and trace minerals that are mostly fed to the brood to safeguard the life-cycle of the colony. Honey bees search high and wide for the best flowers, and once located they return to the hive and communicate to the other bees where the flowers are. Foraging is the most dangerous time for the worker and it takes its toll. They can be eaten by birds and other insects, rained on, become chilled as dusk approaches and die before they return. Recall from Chapter 2, workers often die, working diligently until the very end.

What is Bee 'Dancing?

Once the honey bee scout makes an encouraging find, she drinks up, packs the pollen onto her sacs, and takes flight. As she returns her brightly bulging legs are a glorious vision to behold. She can't harvest all of it herself, and sharing and collecting the yield will require a lot of help (See Photo Image 4. 2 Forager Returning to the Hive). When she arrives to the hive the news of her discovery will be shared through dance. This dance is so remarkably communicative that it often gets called a language. The role of the waggle dance in this sophisticated system of communication is primarily to direct the colony's foraging effort toward nectar and pollen producing flowers.

Photo Image 4.2: Forager Returning to the Hive
Notice her brightly packed and colourful pollen sacs, and her sisters anticipating her return
Credit: Emily Skeels/Shutterstock

Successful foragers perform the dance within the hive to recruit their sisters to a profitable food source (Thom et al., 2007). By closely following a dancer, potential recruits acquire information about the location and the abundance of the food source. The source's direction and whether it yields nectar and/or pollen, water, or a potential new nest-site location will be conveyed through one of two specific dances; the Round dance and Waggle dance. Let's begin with the Round Dance.

The **Round Dance**, as the name indicates, is a circular movement. It is used to point out a food source that is less than 50 meters (165 feet) from the hive. It is considered the simplest dance as it does not communicate precise distance or directional information. It merely informs the workers that there is a food source within close proximity. Yet, even before the returning forager performs her dance, she will regurgitate the nectar she had sucked up into her crop, and place it either directly into a honey comb or exchange the food with other inside workers; a process referred to as **trophallaxis,** or trophallactic interaction (See Photo Image 4.3: Trophallaxis).

Trophallaxis

Trophallaxis or food sharing is when two workers share the crop content (a mix of nectar and other substances) that has been stored (Winston, 1987; Korst & Velthuis, 1982). It begins when one worker begs for food or another worker offers it. A begging bee pushes its proboscis (tongue) towards the mouth of another bee. The other bee then opens its mandibles, pushes its proboscis forward and

regurgitates a drop of nectar from its crop, which the begging bee takes (Korst & Velthuis, 1982). The offering bee will regurgitate a drop of nectar and offer it to another bee. As a result the colony's adult foragers' crops will contain the same mix of nectar. Korst and Velthuis's (1982) research noted that there is a tendency for food to pass from older to younger bees.

See Photo Image 4.3: Trophallaxis
⬡ Notice the various larvae floating in royal jelly and others in honey.
⬡ What day in their larva growth will workers no longer be fed royal jelly?
Credit: Inventori/Thinkstock

Once the exchange of food is completed, she will gain her sisters' attention by crawling on top of them whilst she begins her dance. In fact if you were observing a hive, it is easy to notice how the workers will stop their activities and turn their attention toward her judiciously observing her as she makes each dance revolution. If the forager considers the food source to be abundant, her enthusiastic 'dance' (waggling abdomen) could leave one with the impression she is running in a circle (Winston, 1987). The dancing forager may leave thereafter, while the other foragers drink honey (energy) to prepare for their flight, and then they too will exit the hive. They in turn will bring back more pollen and nectar and spread the word, until the hive is finally full, or the food source is depleted.

If however, the scout's food source is a farther than 50 meters (165 feet) from the hive, the forager will perform the **Waggle Dance**. It involves a type of shivering side-to-side motion of the abdomen that could consist of as many as one or up to a hundred or more circuits involving two phases: the waggle phase and the return phase (See Illustration 4.1: Honeybee Waggle Dance). A worker's waggle dance involves running through a small figure-eight pattern (Amdam & Omholt, 2003; Blackiston, 2015; Buchmann, 2005). This is a more multifaceted dance than the round dance, as it provides a precise visual map; including information regarding direction, distance, and quality of a the resource (such as food or a nesting sites). Researchers have been able to map the distance and location where bees forage from month to month by measuring the angle of the dance in relation to the sun while she moves in a figure-eight pattern. The hive's honeycombs are built vertically, so straight up means toward the sun, and down means away from the sun, and so on. The bee will perform the dance by aligning her body in the exact direction of where the food is in accordance with the sun. It is the angle that communicates direction. The more enthusiastically she shakes her abdomen, the more abundant the bounty.

For instance, the angle to 12 o'clock represents the angle to fly with respect to the sun. If the bee ran from 6 to 12 o'clock, i.e. straight up, this would say *"fly directly towards the sun"*. If 7 to 1 o'clock, it would mean *"fly just to the right of the sun"* and 12 to 6 o'clock *"fly directly away from the sun"*, and the dance pattern will begin to look like a figure-eight, as the bee repeats the straight part of the movement every time it circles back to the center area again. In other words the bees translate the angle to the sun as an angle to the vertical. The more times she repeats her movements (longer the dance), the father away the distance from the hive to the food source (See Illustration 4.1: Honeybee Waggle Dance).

After completing her waggle dance, she may once again share part of the food source with the other bees. It's assumed they do this so they can communicate details about the food's quality from that particular location. So a bee will 'say' to its sisters *'fly over there for about 2 mile and you will find something that tastes like this'*. Workers will retain this information for several days, and they will adjust their foraging times to align when the food is available. They may even form cognitive maps of their surroundings. A **cognitive map** is a mental representation of physical space (American Psychological Association, 2002). The honey bee is unlikely to make many repeat visits if a plant

provides little in the way of reward.   A single worker will visit different flowers in the morning if there is sufficient attraction and reward in a particular kind of flower. Her foraging will continue unless the plants stop producing reward, or if poor weather conditions arise. Remember rain is dangerous for the honey bee (Blackiston, 2015; Buchmann, 2005). However, over time researchers have continued to investigate the dances, and through their research knowledge has been gleaned that indicates pheromones also have a role to play.

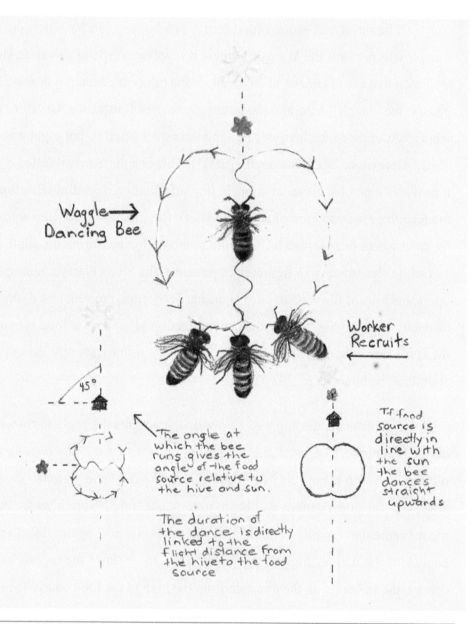

Illustration 4.1: Honeybee Waggle Dance
  The angle from sun indicates direction, and duration of waggle signifies distance
Credit: Bake

Pheromones: An Important Part of the Dance Communication

Pheromones are a chemical substance produced and released into the environment by an animal, especially a mammal or an insect, which affects the behaviour or functioning of others of its species. Honey bees have one of the most complex pheromonal communication systems found in nature, possessing 15 known glands that produce an array of compounds (Boch & Shearer, 1971; Moritz & Burgin, 1987).

All three of the honey bees secreted these chemical messengers and they will be received by the bee's antenna and other body parts (Tew, 2015; Warton et. al., 2007; Winston, 1987). Among many of its pheromones, the honey bee will release a volatile substance when attacked or frightened by a predator that can trigger aggression in members of the same species. And as you may know bees are famous for many things, including their ability to inflict painful stings. Honey bees do not randomly attack however, they only do when they feel the need to defend their colony, or if they are seriously disturbed outside the hive (Boch & Shearer, 1971; Crane, 1990).

Information is often transferred by scent in honey bee colonies. Thom, Gilley, Hooper, and Esch (2007), conducted research to determine whether or not waggle dancers produced a scent that distinguishes them from the non-dancing foragers. Their results indicated that dancers did in fact produce four hydrocarbons that distinguish them from non-dancing foragers, and, when these hydrocarbons were blown into the hive, foraging activity increased, as noted by a greater number of bees that left the hive after a dance occurred (Thom et al., 2007).

Although Thom et al.'s, (2007), experiments revealed that the waggle dance scent increased the number of foragers that left the hive, the exact mechanism underlying the effect is still unclear. Given the function of the waggle dance scent, these researchers proposed that the scent which was fanned onto the dance floor in their experiments, attracted potential recruits to the dance floor, thereby increasing the probability of encounters between potential recruits and dancers, and finally the number of recruits. Under conditions that would naturally unfold in the hive (without human fanning manipulation), the scent would originate from the dancers themselves, who would also use a fanning technique to mark not only the dance floor, but the individual dancers (Thom et al., 2007).

Honey Bee Fanning

All bees participate in the act of fanning to control the temperature and humidly of the hive. During the warm months and particularly honey production season, groups of bees line the entrance facing the hive and fan energetically to draw air into the hive. They rely on fresh air to help maintain a constant temperature of 33-35 degrees Celsius (93 to 95 degrees Fahrenheit) to safely raise the developing brood (Blackiston, 2015). Fanning also accelerates the evaporation of excess moisture from the nectar. Once the honey is gooey enough, the bees seal off the cell of the honeycomb with wax. In one year, a colony of bees eats between 120 and 200 pounds of honey.

Bee fanning is also part of communication. As you might recall from the examination of the honey bees anatomy, bees have a scent gland located at the end of their abdomen called the Nasonov gland (Dyer, 2002). As foragers enter the hive, they will arch their abdomen, fan their wings and release a sweet scent into the air. This pheromone is extremely stimulating and appealing to bees, and as noted earlier it serves as an orientation message to returning foragers. As Blackiston wrote, "Come hither... this is your hive and where you belong" (2015, p. 33). Beekeepers will also purchase synthetic queen bee pheromone and use this chemical to lure swarms of bees into a trap, or to capture their own swarming bees to establish a new hive.

Bees use many odour cues from the food source to communicate crucial details. A number of researchers believe that honey bees carry the unique smells of the flowers they have visited on their bodies.

Fun Fact: Researchers used a robotic bee that was programmed to do the waggle dance talk. They observed that the recruits (followers) were able to fly in the correct direction and distance, but they were unable to find the correct source of food. However, once the robotic bee had a floral odour applied to it, the bees were able to pinpoint the flowers (Marshall, 2011).

It is at this point in the chapter we turn our attention to flowers and pollination, which is an immensely important talent. Consider the fact that bees supply our homes with beautiful bouquets of flowers, an abundance of food choices, and their pollination handiwork is estimated to be over US$200 billion annually worldwide (Gallai et al., 2009). The agriculture industry can't flourish without them.

The Scholarship of Pollination

The scholarship of pollination includes many disciplines, such as botany, ecology, entomology and horticulture. One of the most eminent scientists to study flowers was Charles Darwin, who

Charles Darwin.

overtime would expand the scientific understanding of pollination. For instance, following the 1859, publication of Darwin famous book, *The Origin of Species*, in 1862, he published, *The Various Contrivances by which Orchids Are Fertilized by Insects*. In this text Darwin demonstrated how several orchid flowers had evolved elaborate structures by natural selection in order to facilitate cross-pollination. He also suggested that orchids and their insect pollinators evolved by interacting with one another over many generations ~ a process referred to as coevolution. Darwin's studies of pollination would propagate, and in 1876, he wrote a book on pollination biology, *The Effects of Cross and Self Fertilization in the Vegetable Kingdom*.

See Photo Image 4.4: Charles Darwin
Credit: Nicku/Shutterstock

Charles Darwin however was not the first to study fertilization. The discovery of sex in plants arose in 1694, when Rudolf Jakob Camerarius (1665-1721) a German botanist and physician empirically demonstrated that plants reproduce sexually. Camerarius discovered the fact that specific part of a flower had various roles to play in seed production. While studying certain bisexual species of flowers; plants that had both male and female reproductive organs, he noted that a stamen (male pollen-producing organ) and a pistil (female ovule-producing organ) were both required for seed production. Several fertile minds would continue this scientific study, and decades later Christian Konrad Sprengel (1750 – 1816), would be the first to recognize that the function of flowers was to attract insects and that nature favoured cross-pollination ~ thus the pollination process, and the vital interaction between flower and pollen.

It is perhaps a sobering and humbling fact to consider, that although even today as we bring together decades of scientific knowledge that informs us on how to provide our plants the proper temperature, type of soil, amount of water and sunlight, that without the bee's involvement ~ their pollination ~ all of our work is literally fruitless. It is therefore behooves us to explore the pollination and fertilization process, and the honey bee's role. To begin you will be introduced to the historical reasoning behind the use of Latin names for plants, followed by the anatomy of the flower.

Plants ~ *Why Latin Names?*

Plants (and animals), are given Latin names because believe it or not, it was and continues to be done to make life easier. Latin is the international language of **natural science**, and Latin names and terminology are understood by naturalists worldwide. For example a French, German and English botanist will all understand each other if talking about Papaver rhoeas, whereas it would take time to translate their subject of interest if they were using the terms, Pavot Rouge, Klatschmohm and Field Poppy, respectively (See Photo Image 4.5: Papaver rhoeas).

Photo Image 4.5: Papaver Rhoeas
Credit: olm26250/Thinkstock

All formally recognized plant species are given a binomial Latin name the first time they are described formally in a scientific publications. If for some reason the name is later revised or changed in any way, this change must be formally published as well. Names are given by botanists who specialize in plant taxonomy (Arteca, 2015). Although there are many authorities for plant names, "L." is in fact a scientifically recognized abbreviation for Carl Linnaeasu (1707-1778), the Swedish naturalist who introduced the Latin binomial system for naming of plants and animals (See Photo Image 4. 6: The Carl Linnaeus Statue, Stockholm, Sweden).

Recall, *Apis* is Latin for "bee". As such it should be noted that in 1758, **entomologist** Robert Snodgrass affirmed that the correct usage is to use two words, i.e. honey and bee, since we are describing a type of bee.

Fun Fact: This explains why this author has used two words ~ honey bee throughout this text. And to further respect the work of many naturalist and botanist, the honey bee, not honeybee, is the listed common name in the Integrated Taxonomic Information System, the Entomological Society of America Common Names of Insects Database, and the Tree of Life Web Project. See Chapter Activities to continue to explore this specialized and fascinating topic.

Photo Image 4.6: The Carl Linnaeus Statue, Stockholm, Sweden.
Credit: ppl /Shutterstock

Anatomy of a Flower

Flowers provide one of the most dependable external characteristics for establishing relationships among plant identification (angiosperm species). Angiosperm means a plant that produces seeds within an enclosure (See Illustration 4.2: Anatomy of a Flower).

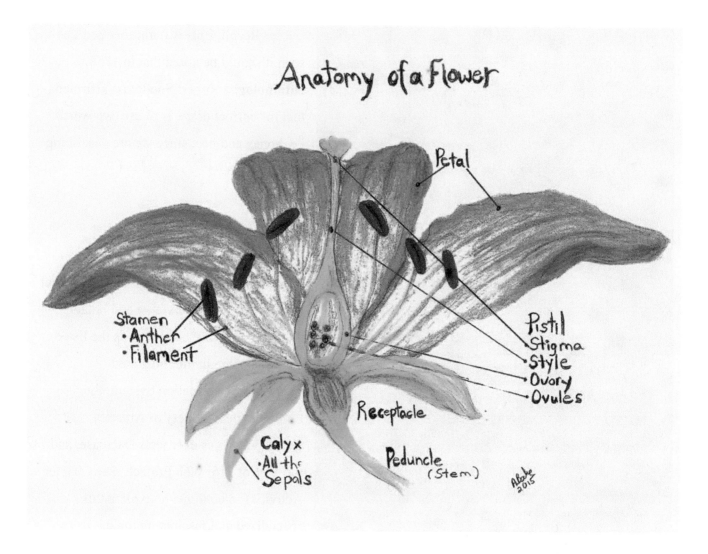

Illustration 4.2: Anatomy of a Flower
Credit: Bake, 2015

The term "angiosperm" comes from the Greek composite word (angeion, "case" or "casing", and sperma, "seed") meaning "enclosed seeds", which describes the enclosed condition of the seeds (Palmer et al., 2004). Angiosperm contrasts with the gymnosperms, a term that comes from the Greek words that mean naked seed. Gymnosperms are seed plants that have an ovule that is not enclosed in a carpel, as is the case in angiosperms. The ovule instead forms on a leaf-like structure and are frequently amassed into compound structures that are often cone-shaped, hence the colloquial name for some of the group: conifers" (Christenhusz, et al., 2011; Palmer et al., 2004).

A typical flower consists of four major parts. However a walk through any garden will reveal that there are countless variations in arrangements, structure and modification of these basic parts. For simplicity see Illustration 4.1: Parts of a Flower, where you will quickly observe the four main parts; the sepals, petals, stamens and pistils. At the top the flower stem widens, and because it holds all the floral parts together it is called the **receptacle**. Attached to it are circlets of leaf-like structures usually green (sometimes brown) called **sepals** beneath the petals, collectively the sepals are called the **calyx**. The calyx serves to protect the flower and its reproductive organs, which is necessary for the continuation of the plant. In many flowers, sepals are modified in various ways or even completely missing. For example, some plants have calyx that contain spines which deter animals form feeding on them. **Petals** are the brightly coloured part of the flower that are used to attracted pollinators. About 80 percent of flowers are **hermaphrodites** (or perfect flowers), which is a term used in botany to describe plants that have both male and female reproductive organs. Conversely those having only male reproductive organs or only female reproductive organs are called imperfect flowers, or unisexual flowers.

Stamen ~ The Male Reproductive Part of the Flowers

The **Stamen** represents the male reproductive part of the flowers. A stamen consists of two main parts; the **Filament** which is attached at the base of the flower and it supports the anther. The

Anther produces the flower's sticky powder ~ Pollen. Pollen is the male reproductive cells, or sperm, which fertilizes the ovules and provides the male gamete (See Photo Image 4.7: A Lily Stamen with Pollen ~ Lilium).

The function and form of stamens and pistils are remarkably varied. For instance, filaments can be hairy or smooth, short or long, thick or thin. Anthers may be slightly visible or highly elaborate and enlarged. For instance, the passion flower (Passiflora incarnate) comes in a variety of colours, and the anthers' are always vividly coloured.

Photo Image 4.7: A Lily Stamens with Pollen (Lilium)
Credit: Watcha/Thinkstock

Recap: **Stamen** = Filament + Anther ~ Memory Tip Sta**MEN**

Pistil ~ The Female Reproductive Part of a Flower

The **pistil** is the female reproductive parts of a flower. The **pistil** is the collective term for the carpel(s). It has four key parts, the stigma, a style, ovary and ovules. The **stigma** is the top part of the pistil and it is supported by the style. It is often sticky and it receives the pollen (male sperm) during the fertilization process. (See Photo Image 4.8: The Tulip ~ *Tulipa*). The Tulip's pistil is visible, and

surrounded by the stamens. The style is the tube the joins the stigma and ovary, and the **ovary** sits at the base and contains the ovules or eggs. Each ovule has a female **gamete.**

Photo Image 4.8: The Tulip ~ *Tulipa*
Credit: Richard Griffin/Thinkstock

Recap: **Pistil** = Stigma + Style + Ovary

Pollination and Fertilization

Sex, Sex, Sex
The Jack-in-the-pulpit is considering a sex change.
The violets have a secret, the dandelion is smug. The daffodils are obsessive. The orchid is finally satisfied, having produce over a million seeds. The bellflower is not satisfied and is slowly bending its stigma in order to reach its own pollen. The pansies wait expectantly, their vulviform faces lifted to the sky. The evening primrose is interested in one thing and one thing only. A stroll through the garden is almost embarrassing. (Russell, 2001, p.46)

Flowers are the structures of flowering plants that contain the specialized parts needed for sexual reproduction (Arteca, 2015). Pollination is crucial to the flowering plant's life cycle, and it is part of the sexual reproduction process which results in seeds that grow into new plants. Plants have **gametes**, which contain half the number of chromosomes for that plant species. Male gametes are found inside tiny pollen grains on the anthers of flowers. Female gametes are found in the ovules of a flower. The pollination process brings the male and female gametes together.

Pollinium (plural ~ pollinia), is a mass of pollen grains in a plant that are produced in the plant's anther, and transferred during pollination as a single element; a pollen grain (Arteca, 2015; Winston, 2014). Each anther can carry up to 100,000 grains of pollen, so it's quite a prolific substance. Pollen on its own can't get from the anthers to the ovules, therefore it relies on other things to move the pollen for pollination to occur. As you know, flowers come in a dazzling assortment of sizes, shapes and colours, and their sweet nectar and nourishing pollen which encourage many animal pollinators including birds, bats, beetles, butterflies, and bees to visit and pollinate them. Plants also tend to have their scent output at maximal levels only when the flowers are ready for pollination (Scientific American, 2005). Once a flower has been sufficiently pollinated, quantitative and/or qualitative changes to the floral bouquets lead to a poorer attractiveness which helps direct pollinators to unpollinated flowers instead (Scientific American, 2005).

Wind-pollinated flowers also exist, and their pollen grains are shaped to make it easy for the wind to pick them up and deposit them. There petals are generally small, often brown or dull green, since they really have no requirement to attract insects. And unlike pollinated plants they have no scent, or nectar. This concept will be discussed later in this chapter.

For the most part however, the world requires the type of pollination that is only accomplished by bees. It is an inescapable fact; bees' value to natural ecosystems as pollinators is incalculable. Bees are easily seen visiting flowers and collecting their sweet nectar. As they do, they pick up pollen from the male's anther and deposit it on the stigmas. Only after the pollen has landed on the stigma of a suitable flower of the same species, can a chain of events happen that provides fertilization to occur and the making of a seed(s).

In pollination, a male pollen grain lands on a sticky stigma. The grain absorbs moisture, then it swells, cracks and sprouts a pollen tube. The male sperm (pollen) has two nuclei. The first will form a pollen tube which will pierce the stigma and burrow down within the style toward the ovary (Russell, 2001).

Illustration 4.3: Fertilization
Credit: Bake, 2015

The generative nucleus in the pollen grain divides and releases two male gametes, which move down the pollen tube. This pollen tube will carry its two gametes towards the ovules in the ovary to meet a female gamete. The pollen grain **haploid** has half of the DNA (genetic information) that is needed to make a new plant. One male gamete cell will fuse with the ovum, producing zygote. The second male gamete fuses with the two polar bodies located in the center of sac, producing the endosperm tissue that will provide energy for the embryo's growth. When the two gametes join and their chromosomes (DNA) combine fertilization has transpired, and

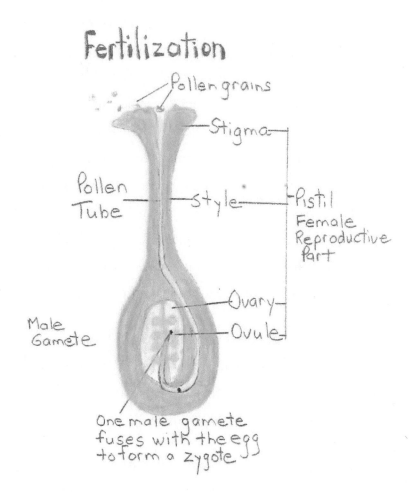

fertilized cell now contains a normal complement of chromosomes (Russell, 2001; Valayamghat, 1997). This zygote will form an embryo inside the ovule. The rest of the ovule forms endosperm (food for the germinating seed). The ovaries become fruit, and the ovule forms the testa (hard, dry, protective layer); the mature ovule = seed.

An ovary contains one or more ovules. After fertilization, the ovule develops into a seed in the ovary, which contains a food store and an embryo that will later grow into a new plant. The ovary develops into a fruit to protect the seed. Some flowers, such as avocados have only one ovule in their ovary, so their fruit only has one seed. Other flowers, for instance kiwi, has lots of ovules in their ovary, so their fruit contains many seeds (See Photo Image 4.9: Kiwifruit and Avocados).

Photo Image 4.9: Kiwi fruit and Avocados
⬡ One ovule or many ovules will determine the number of potential seeds
Credit: Thinkstock/Xanya69

About 80 percent of flowers are hermaphrodites; both male and female. Hermaphrodites flowers could easily pollinate and fertilize themselves, but most don't, instead they try to mix and match their pollen and eggs with the flowers and eggs from flowers of the same species. Sex, good-sex is all about **Cross-pollination** (Russell, 2001). Cross-pollination produces stronger plants. But plants must still be of the same species. For example, only pollen from a daisy can pollinate another daisy, so pollen from a rose would not work. For cross pollination to occur, it's much more effective if you they get insects to do their bidding, and as you can imagine an outrageous beautiful and sweet smelling flower can attract lots of insects.

As the honey bee labours in the garden, foraging from flower to flower, slurping up its nectar, the flower's pollen sticks to its furry body, so it begs the question... what will she do with it? This is where the content from Chapter 3: Honey Bee Anatomy becomes clear. The worker will use her front two legs to wipe the pollen from her body into a sticky mass, and stick it on the inside of her back legs. The bee then uses its back legs to compress the pollen further while she moves the little masses of pollen into the corbicula on each leg. Once she is full she will then return to its hive. The pollen will then be deposited into an appropriate cell. The hive needs pollen to make its bee bread, which will be the product of pollen, mixed with honey, and secretions from the brood nurse bees. Once the process is completed it will be stored in honey combs. Bee bread is essential to the colony's survival, as it is fed to the larvae, and, the newly emerged worker bees must eat it because bee bread supports the development of their glands that produce food for the larvae and the queen.

Recap: Bee Bread = honey + pollen + secretions from the brood nurse bees

The second type of pollination is **self-pollination**. Most self-pollinating plants have small, relatively inconspicuous flowers that shed pollen directly onto the stigma, and sometimes even before the bud opens. Self-pollination is ecologically advantageous under certain circumstances because self-pollinators do not need to be visited by animals to produce seed. As a result these plants expend less energy in the production of pollinator attractants. They can also grow in areas where the kinds of insects or other animals that might visit them are absent or very scarce, for instance in high elevations (See Photo Image: Pine Branch with Buds). Among plants that can self-pollinate are peas, sunflowers and many varieties of orchids (Russell, 200; Valayamghat, 1997). It is now time to take a closer look at pollen (See Chart 4.1: Review of Bee and Wind Pollination).

Chart 4.1: Review of Bee and Wind Pollination	
Honey Bee Pollinated	**Wind Pollinated**
• Honey bees are most active at temperatures between 16 degrees C. (60 DF) & 41 degrees C. (105 DF) • Winds above 15 miles per hour reduce their activity and stop it completely at about 25 miles per hour	• Don't need to attract insects or birds • Normally flower in early spring before their leaves arrive develop so they do not block the breeze and prevent pollination
Examples *Trees*: Almond, Cherry, Apple *Crops*: Blueberry, Clover, Squash, Sunflower	**Examples** *Trees*: Firs, Spruce, **Pine** *Crops*: Soybean, Wheat, Corn, Rye, Barley, Strawberry
• Often sweetly scented contain nectar • Large, brightly coloured petals	• No scent No nectar • Inconspicuous and Drab, • Small petals, dull green in colour
Moderate quantity of pollen • Less excess than wind pollination	Pollen produced in great quantities • Large percentage does not reach another flower
Pollen often sticky or spiky • Stick to bees & other insects	Pollen light and smooth • Blown in the wind
Plant's Anthers located inside flower • To brush against insects	Plant's Anthers dangle • To release pollen into the wind
Stigma inside the flower • Insects can brush against it	Generally large stigma that hangs outside the flower to catch the drifting pollen
Photo Image:Pine Branch with Buds *Credit*: scisettialfio/Thinkstock	

"Pollen….. The Hidden Sexuality of Flowers"
Kesseler & Harley

Hopefully by this point in the chapter the examination of pollination and fertilization was enough to convince you that pollen is more than just something that gets up your nose or stains your table cloths. Pollen is a flower's method of making more flowers, which provides plants and human society genetic diversity. Perhaps we don't think about it often, but most of the vegetables, fruits, and nuts in our shopping carts exist because a bee was in the right place at the right time. Domesticated *or managed*; the honey bee, and wild bees pollinate more than 16 percent of the world's flowering plant species, and about 400 of its agricultural crops. Without bees around to do their thing, certain plants might vanish, as would the birds, mammals, and insects that also depend on those plants for food. It's not just about us humans and the foods we need and love.

The study of pollen grains is called **micropaleontology**. Pollen is miniscule; real small, but today, with the assistance of technology pollen grains can be more meticulously viewed and they will tell us which floral species it came from. Even the same species of plant looks differently if it was grown in different region of the world. Jonathan Drori stated, "all plants have a "different pollen

signature, if you like, or a different pollen fingerprint. By looking at the proportions and combinations of different kinds of pollen in a sample, you can tell very precisely where it came from" (2010, TedTalk).

Many plants and trees tend to have boring flowers, so wind pollination is important. Wind pollinators (also called Anemophily), also differ in structure compared to insect pollinated flowers.

Photo Image 4:10 Pine Pollen
Credit: De Romija/ Shutterstock

Anemophily is an adaptation that helps to separate the male and female reproductive systems of a single plant, reducing the effects of inbreeding (Shukla, Vijayaraghavan, and Chaudhry, 1998). Wind pollinators tend to disperse a large amount of pollen to ensure their pollen has a chance of reaching another plant of the same species (Angel, 2016). One example is the pine ~ Latin, Pinus (See Photo Image 4: 1 Pine Pollen). It's large and feathery stigma can easily snare airborne pollen grains.

Many grasses and trees are also wind pollinated, which include nearly all conifers such as, spruces and pine. Since tree anemophilous pollen grains are meant to be carried by the wind, structurally it is very light and smooth - so it can be easily blown without clumping together.

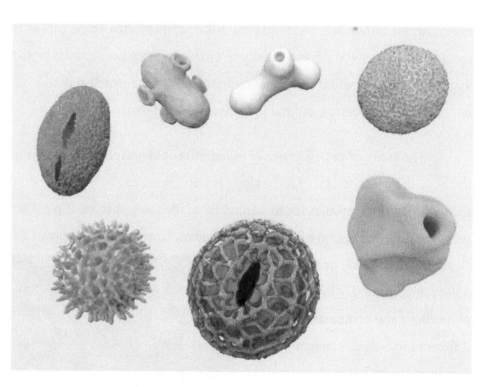

Apart from the amazing colour diversity and beauty, a pollen grain can also convey what species it came from and where the plant was grown (See Photo Image 4.11: Pollen Diversity).

Photo Image 4.11: Pollen Diversity
Pollen grains from various plants
Credit: De Juan Gaertner/Shutterstock

If you are as student interested in the field of policing and or forensic science, you might want to consider the contribution pollen has made in these professional fields. To date, New Zealand is a world leader in forensic palynology/pollen. Their key organization is The Forensic Group which was established in 2008. To quote their website, "Pollen is a form of trace evidence (trace material being that which is present in small but measurable amounts or that is microscopic in size – this may also include fibres, hair, glass, etc.). The main forensic application of pollen analysis is assisting to prove or disprove a link between people and objects with places or with other people (http://www.theforensicgroup.co.nz/expertise/pollen/). Pollen has a rich story to teach, and perhaps on some level it has peeked your academic interests or curiously.

Let's take a moment and absorb the facts of this chapter, and as we do so let's return to the hive and the moment the waggling forager arrives with a story to share. The next time you are outside, whether in your neighborhood or a walk in nature, consider heeding the advice of the waggle dance honey bee observers… *slow down, focus, pay attention and be present.*

CHAPTER REVIEW QUESTIONS

1. Let's change it up a bit. How many parts of the flower's anatomy can you identify?

A. _____

B. _____

C. _____

D. _____

E. _____

F. _____

G. _____

H. _____

I. _____

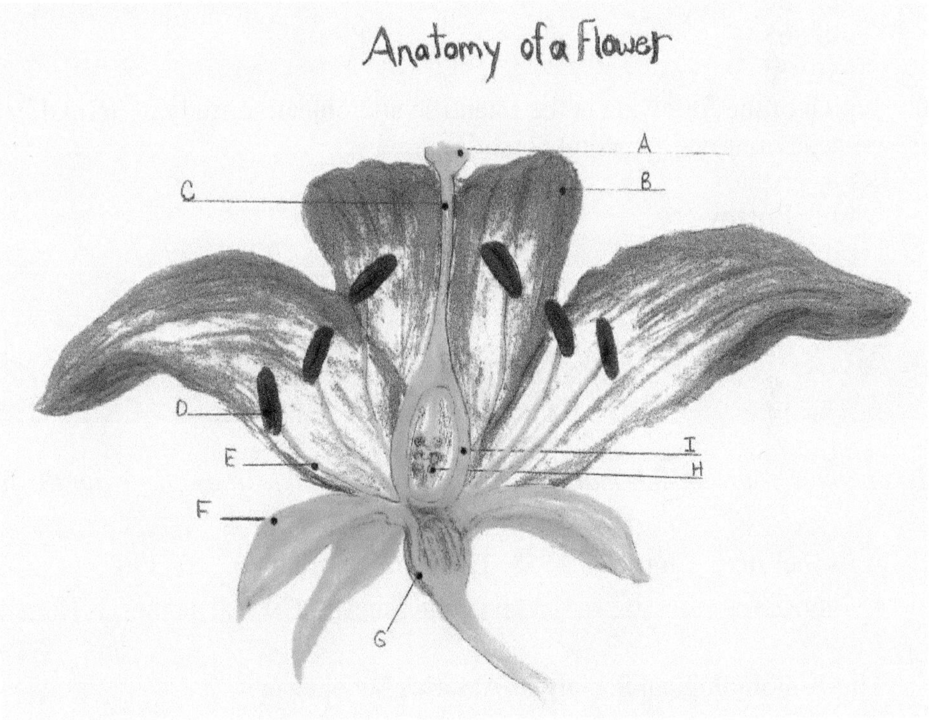

Anatomy of a Flower

2. Who was the first to study fertilization, and in the process demonstrated that plants reproduce sexually?
    a. Charles Darwin
    b. Karl von Frisch
    c. Carl Linnaeus
    d. Rudolf Jakob Camerarius

3. Who wrote, The Various Contrivances by which Orchids Are Fertilized by Insects?
   a. Charles Darwin
   b. Karl von Frisch
   c. Carl Linnaeus
   d. Rudolf Jakob Camerarius

4. Who was the first to discover that non-human animals possess a symbolic means of communication?
   a. Charles Darwin
   b. Karl von Frisch
   c. Carl Linnaeus
   d. Rudolf Jakob Camerarius

5. The Round Dance, as the name indicates, is a circular movement. It is used to point out a food source that is less than how many meters from the hive?
   a. 50
   b. 55
   c. 60
   d. 65

6. Which of the following is the scientific and objective study of animal behaviour, with an emphasis on behaviour under natural conditions?
   a. Apiary
   b. Botany
   c. Ethology
   d. Physiology

Activities

To enhance your understanding and nurture your curiosities check out the following:

I. Apis mellifera Linnaeus, 1758. Taxonomic Serial No.: 154396
   - https://www.itis.gov/servlet/SingleRpt/SingleRpt?search_topic=TSN&search_value=154396#null

II. The "Entomological Society of America Webpagae
   - http://www.entsoc.org/policy-initiatives

III. Go to the following website and type in your favourite house and garden plant to discover its Latin name.
   - http://entsoc.org/common-names
   - 2017 Document that lists the Insects and Related Organisms Sorted by Common Names
   - http://entsoc.org/sites/default/files/files/common_name.pdf

IV. Charles Darwin, online version of THE EFFECTS OF CROSS & SELF-FERTILISATION IN THE VEGETABLE KINGDOM
   - http://charles-darwin.classic-literature.co.uk/the-effects-of-cross-and-self-fertilisation/

V. Robert Evans Snodgrass Papers, 1920s-1963, preserved with the Smithsonian Institution Archives
   - These papers consist mostly of notes, sketches and drawings from Robert Evans Snodgrass's entomological research. Also included are occasional photographs, correspondence, and manuscripts.
   - https://siarchives.si.edu/collections/siris_arc_217854

VI. The Canadian Pollination Initiative
   - Is one of nine new Strategic Networks announced in September 2009[2] and supported by the Natural Sciences and Engineering Research Council of Canada (NSERC)
   - http://www.nserc-crsng.gc.ca/index_eng.asp

KEY TERMS

Anthecology
- Is the study of pollination as well as the relationships between flowers and their pollinators

Aryan
- The term was adopted as a racial category through the work of Arthur de Gobineau
- Gobineau's ideology of race was based on an idea of blonde northern European "Aryans" who had migrated across the world and founded all major civilizations

Coevolution
- The influence of closely associated species on each other in their evolution
- In biology, it occurs when two or more species reciprocally affect each other's evolution

Cognitive map
- Is a mental representation of physical space

Gametes
- A mature haploid male or female germ cell that is able to unite with another of the opposite sex in sexual reproduction to form a zygote

Haploid
- A cell or nucleus having a single set of unpaired chromosomes

Natural Science
- A branch of science that deals with the physical world, e.g., physics, chemistry, geology, and biology

Ethology
- Is the scientific and objective study of animal behaviour, with an emphasis on behaviour under natural conditions, and viewing behaviour as an evolutionarily adaptive trait

Karl von Frisch
- An Austrian ethologist who among many achievements was one of the first to translate the meaning of the honey bee waggle dance

Pheromones: pher·o·mone (ferə͵mōn)
- A chemical substance produced and released into the environment by an animal, especially a mammal or an insect, affecting the behaviour or physiology of others of its species

Round Dance
- A term used in beekeeping and ethology, that describes the honey bees dance, which is a short version of the honey bee waggle dance, and indicates that a food source is nearby (typically less than 10–20 m from the hive)

The Entomological Society of America (ESA)
- Is the largest organization in the world serving the professional and scientific needs of entomologists and individuals in related disciplines
- Founded in 1889, has over 6,000 members affiliated with educational institutions, health agencies, private industry, and government.
- Members are researchers, teachers, extension service personnel, administrators, marketing representatives, research technicians, consultants, students, pest management professionals, and hobbyists.

Sensory Physiology
- Is the study of seeing, hearing, feeling, smelling, tasting, and the sense of balance, and the way in which biological mechanisms convert physical events

Trophallaxis
- Food sharing is when two worker share the crop content (a mix of nectar and other substances that has been stored

Waggle Dance
- A term used in beekeeping and ethology, that describes the honey bee's dance which is based on a figure-eight. This dance indicates that food is at a distance farther way from the hive

Chapter 4: Review and Study Notes

Chapter 4: Review and Study Notes

Chapter 5: Beekeeping

"The bee is more honoured than other animals, not because she labours,
but because she labours for others".

~ St John Chrysostom ~
The Archbishop of Constantinople from 347 to 407 ~

CHAPTER OBJECTIVES

After reading this chapter you should be able to:

1. Appreciate the Tree's Value to Earth and Humans
2. Explain queen rearing and its history
3. Describe large scale migratory commercial beekeeping
4. Discuss the economic impact of commercial beekeeping
5. Identify and describe the beekeeping equipment required for hobby or back yard beekeepers

Introduction

We begin where Chapter 4 concluded, pollination and plants, and in doing so we must tip our hats to trees. It isn't just the brilliantly coloured aromatic flowering plants that have pollen. Often when visualizing a busy bee we imagine them in our gardens, foraging from flower-to-flower and unwittingly pollinating our plants. But the bee-tree relationship is responsible for a huge selection of products and nutritional food. To achieve this task a large amount of nectar and pollen must be gathered from numerous flowering trees, and as you will soon discover tree pollination is big business.

The benefits derived from the bee-tree pollination process are critical, but trees also supply us with two of life's essentials, food and oxygen, and their importance has been celebrated for hundreds of years. In Chapter 6 you will be introduced to key environmental advocates, and in particular the history of Arbor Day which took root decades ago, to become an annual global day set aside to recognize the need to plant and care for trees.

And although honey bees' pollinate countless plant species whose existence would be endangered without them, trees also matter to bees. Wise beekeepers can well afford to take the time to plant trees along their roads and around their homes and apiaries, for the bee benefits from shade, and as the tree grows older it becomes an important factor in the life of the bee.

Before we begin our examination of tree pollination and commercial beekeeping let's play homage to the tree, and its relationship with humans and planet Earth.

Trees, Earth and Humans

A tree's value is immeasurable, and the health and welfare of planet Earth depends on them. Trees help preserve our soil by reducing erosion and by creating a soil climate suitable for microorganism to grow. A tree's hollow is also a great home for wild bees and other animals. Humans use their shade for picnics, and their branches to hang our swings and birdhouses. Throughout history artists have painted their majesty and today's real estate agents know a healthy mature tree can raise a homeowner's property value. Trees are also places of birth and death. They are used as sacred shrines, places of spiritual pilgrimage, and celebration. Although Canada does not have a national tree, the maple leaf has been a Canadian symbol dating back to the 18th century, and it is appears on the coat of arms of parliamentarians and government ministries, the Canadian Forces, Royal Canadian Mounted Police (RCMP), and of course it is depicted on the Canadian flag.

In Canada there are about 180 species of trees (See Photo Image 5.1: National Park Revelstoke in Canada with Boreal Forest). These trees include the large boreal zone that is dominated by coniferous, for instance the pine, spruce and firs, and they all rely on wind-borne pollen or self-pollination (Natural Resources Canada, Canada Centre for Remote Sensing, Research and Development). And when the economic benefits are considered, trees provide a significant financial element.

Trees and their products are essential to the economy. For instance, Canada's forests area is the third-largest in the world, followed by the United States which is ranked 4th. The Canadian forest industry is an export-oriented manufacturing sector, and in 2015, it accounted for almost 7% of all Canadian exports; a total revenue of $32.7 billion (Retrieved on March 30, 2017 from https://www.nrcan.gc.ca/forests/report/economy/16517). Employment opportunities are also created. In 2015, the forest industry employed 201, 645 people, and 9500 of those individuals were from indigenous communities. The Canadian forest industry also makes significant contributions by reducing 25% of all gas emissions (GHGs) each year.

Photo Image 5.1: National Park Revelstoke in Canada with Boreal Forest
Credit: Jiri Kulisek /Shutterstock

In terms of human nourishment, hundreds of food products (fruit, coffee, nuts, etc.) and food additives (for ice cream, chewing gum, etc.) come from trees. Their branches also keep animals, such as birds out of the reach of predators, and many wild animals eat their fruit and leaves for nourishment. And these same leaves provide protective cover for humans as well, and when they fall in autumn they make excellent compost that enriches the soil.

Trees regulate climate by controlling the effects of the sun, rain and wind. Trees filter air by removing dust and absorbing other pollutants like carbon monoxide, sulfur dioxide and nitrogen dioxide. Leaves absorb and filter the sun's radiant energy, keeping things cool in summer. Conversely, trees preserve warmth by providing a screen from harsh wind, and they shield us from the downfall of rain, sleet and hail. Moreover, almost 98% (by weight) of a tree is made up of all six key elements: carbon, hydrogen, oxygen, nitrogen, phosphorus and sulfur; referred to by the acronym, CHNOPS. All these elements are a vital requirement for Life on Earth. Has this list impressed you; hopefully, so feel free to reevaluate the tress around you. Later in this chapter, trees and commercial beekeeping will be discussed.

Beekeeping

Beekeeping, if you recall from Chapter 1, has been recorded since ancient times. Throughout history the various methods used to manage bees has advanced as human societies understanding of bee anatomy, biology and their life cycle developed. In the mid-1800s, innovative insights were made and opportunities forged when L. L. Langstroth invented his hive design. His rectangular bee box design, with its removable wooden frames allowed beekeepers the opportunity to inspect and even remove honey from the honeycomb without terminating the entire colony. This effective and profitable system of beekeeping transformed the field of apiculture and it continues to be the most popular system used by both back yard beekeepers and multimillion dollar commercial beekeeping enterprises.

Queen Rearing

Whether we examine past or present day beekeeping practices, one key detail that inevitably emerges is the need to have a vigorous hive, and the presence of a healthy productive queen bee is vital. To safeguard the well-being of the hive many commercial and hobby beekeepers practice annual requeening, while others only requeen hives when the queen is failing. Requeening regardless of the strategy, a choice and method exists thanks to the early work of **Henry Alley** and **Gilbert M. Doolittle** (See Chapter 1, Chart 1.2: Key Individuals and their Contributions: A Honey Bee Time Line).

In 1861, Henry Alley, William Carey, and E. L. Pratt, all of Massachusetts, began producing queens for sale. These early producers used narrow strips of honeycomb containing eggs and larvae which they fastened to the top bars or to existing partial combs. Then they were added to queenless swarm boxes and the hive would take over, and consequential queen cells would form and be distributed to queenless colonies for mating.

The next step in the evolution of queen rearing was developed by Gilbert M. Doolittle (1846-1918). Doolittle is considered the father of *commercial* queen bee rearing. In 1889, he developed a comprehensive system for rearing queen bees that continues to be the basis for today's modern apiculture, and it has permitted beekeeping to expand from a **cottage industry** to an industrial-scale operation (Blackiston, 2015). Through his research he recognized that larvae could be transfer to artificial wax queen cups. In doing so Doolittle found that he could achieve four important steps; he could raise as many queens as might be needed, replace weak and sickly queens, create new hives, or divide old ones. This accomplishment represented the next phase in creating and supporting sustainable and profitable beekeeping.

Today, queen rearing, or grafting as it is commonly called is considered to simply be the process of transferring larva from the worker cell of the breeder's hive to an artificial queen cell, and this process is undertaken by beekeepers each year. Blackiston writes, "With bees, just like all plants and animals, traits-both good and bad-are passed from one generation to the next…To breed better bees, you need one or more mothers and a whole lot of fathers. So there are two types of colonies you will select to be your breeding stock; queen mothers colony or drone mother colony" (2015, p. 265). Moreover, other bee traits exist that should be considered; gentleness (which is hereditary), resistance to diseases and pest, hardiness, and productively (Blackiston, 2015). Once a beekeeper (or bee breeder) chooses a hive, grafting takes place. The shape of the cell, along with the queenless condition of the hive receiving the newly grafted cells stimulates the workers to feed them a royal jelly diet, which contributes to the development of a queen.

The idea of grafting one's own queen should not inhibit a bee enthusiast's desire to provide a home for our pollinating friends. There are many breeders available to help, as it has become one of the many bee businesses under the umbrella of apiary. Beekeepers today can be categorized into a few groups; a hobby, a sideline operation or a full-time business, with the number of colonies operated varying from one to 30,000. The next section of this chapter will turn to the world of big bee business and examine today's commercial beekeeping.

Migratory Commercial Beekeeping

Similar to all forms of industries, there are various facets of beekeeping that influence how revenue is or can be earned. Income can be generated by the manufacturing and selling of bee keeping equipment. The products produced by the honey bees are also desired goods, for instance, the sale of beeswax, pollen, bee venom, propolis, and royal jelly. These goods however, provide only a minor amount of the industries total gross income. The aspect of commercial beekeeping that really fuels the industry are the sales of honey, production and sale of queen bees and packaged bees, and the renting of colonies for crop pollination. To begin our examination of beekeeping we explore the profession of commercial beekeeping ~ *pollination for sale!*

The distribution of bees for crop pollination is a specialized practice; not a hobby. It is vital to horticulture and agriculture business because fruiting is dependent on fertilization: the result of pollination (See Photo Image 5.2: Small Truck Transporting Beehives). Beekeepers who supply bees for pollination must possess important management skills and knowledge. Knowing how to select strong colonies that are capable of providing the large force of bees needed to do the job is enormously important. In today's agricultural business many farms practice a type of farming called **Mono-cropping.**

Mono-cropping is the agricultural practice of a one-crop economy, where income relies solely on the production and sale of one densely planted crop over a large number of acres. There are many concerns related to this form of farming, and the spread of disease in one. A plant disease would be considered any abnormal condition in plants that interfere with the plant's normal appearance, growth, structure or function (Arteca, 2015). Another challenge arises when the horticulture crop requires insect pollination.

Photo Image 5.2: Small Truck Transporting Beehives
Credit: plastique/Shutterstock

Years of monocrop culture, and the use of herbicides (chemicals used to control weeks), have reduced the amount of natural habitat available to sustain the lives of many pollinating insects (Arteca, 2015). Pollination is vital, thus supplying a pollination service to farmers while each crop is in bloom requires precise timing. Beekeepers and their bees play a critical role in this phase of agriculture in Canada, and all over the world.

Oversight of Canadian agriculture is the responsibility of the department of Agriculture and Agri-Food. Agriculture in Canada is composed of five main agricultural production sectors of commodity production resulting in farm cash receipts from both domestic and for marketing. Of those five areas two specifically require pollination services. In fact of the main five sectors, Canada's agricultural sector is the largest at 34%. This would include grains and oilseeds (wheat, durum, oats, barley, rye, flax seed, canola, soybeans, rice, and corn), and the fourth highest is horticulture at 9%. This agency also oversees Canadian beekeeping operations, because bees are essential to the development of these two sectors.

Canada has over 8,400 beekeepers, with a total of more than 672,000 colonies. According to Agriculture and Agri-Food Canada (2016), the beekeeping industry in Canada is vibrant and flourishing. In 2013, there was a 9% increase in total colonies compared to the average of the previous five years. The majority of honey bee colonies are located in the Prairie Provinces, where long summer days are ideal for foraging. Alberta, Saskatchewan and Manitoba collectively accounted for 84% of Canada's total honey production. In 2013, Canadian honey bee colonies yielded more than 75 million pounds of honey (Katz & Ragoo, 2013).

One might even state that the Canadian honey revenue is pretty sweet. In 2014, honey production's total value was over $176 million, and $50,856,000 (Canadian dollars) was attributed to exports. Interestingly Canada's top honey export destinations were the United States (65%), Japan (33%) and China (3%) (Darrach & Page, 2016).

To Bee or Not to Bee: An Exploration of the Life and Times of the Honey Bee

While honey is the most obvious handiwork of a bee, it is not the most important economically. As mentioned earlier, bees are crucial to the pollination of a host of plants, including fruits, vegetables and crops, such as canola. Canola was by far the most important bee pollinated crop in 2014, with sales topping $7.3 billion. Canada ranks 1st in the world for canola /oil seed rape production. According to the Canola council of Canada, in 2015, there were more than 722,000 honey bee colonies Canada-wide which was an increase from 600,000 in 2000.

Photo Image 5.3: Blooming Canola Field
◉ Skeps in the foreground
Credit: JFsPic/Thinkstock

More than 70% of these colonies are in Western Canada, where canola production has also grown dramatically. About half of a canola plant's flowers are typically visited by honey bees. Bees prefer canola to other flowering plants because they like its colour and scent (Manning & Boland, 2000). Recall that yellow is one of the most attractive colours to a honeybee, along with blue and white (Wilson-Rich, 2014). The fluorescent anthers of canola flowers also make them particularly enticing.

Bees also enjoy foraging in these fields because they don't have to cover large distances when canola is in bloom. Canola field's blossom for relatively long periods, consequently one field can provide bees with a good source of nectar for up to a month (See Photo Image 5.3: Blooming Canola Field).

While commodity canola is primarily wind-pollinated, research indicates that honey bees foraging on canola add to the harvest quantity and quality. Insect pollination is considered a must-have for production of quality hybrid seed. One study showed that the presence of pollinators can increase the germination of resulting seeds from 83% to 96% (Kevan & Eisikowitch, 1990). Estimated contribution of Canadian honey bee pollination to canola crops in 2013 (Canadian dollars) was 1.3 billion dollars (Horticulture and Cross Sectoral Division Agriculture and Agri-Food Canada, 2016).

The canola fields are not the only crop that benefits from bee pollination. In the Canadian agriculture economy, Blueberries placed third with $265 million in sales in 2014. Canada is ranked 2nd in the world in blueberry production, in fact North America produces 75% of the world's blueberries, and Canadian Beekeepers provide around 35,000 colonies of honey bees for blueberry pollination (Government of Canada, 2013-2014). Other crops requiring pollination are apples ($211 million), cranberries ($114 million) and carrots ($94 million). In total, the 2013 economic contribution of honey bee pollination for the production of all fruits and vegetables was estimated to be $562 million.

Bee pollination is not specific to Canada either. In the United States, pollination services have been estimated at over US$200 billion annually around the world (Gallai et al. 2009), which includes the contribution of wild bees to crop productivity (Klein et al., 2007). However, wild insect pollinators have declined in some regions, as agricultural landscapes changed to support the practice of monoculture (Biesmeijer et al. 2006; Potts et al. 2010. Monoculture planting creates an ecosystem and limits the floral diversity and provision of resources for wild pollinators (other bees, birds, butterflies etc.), to survive throughout the season. A major crop pollination goal therefore is to control foraging bees and get them to more effectively visit and pollinate crops.

When examining commercial beekeeping it is the number of bees, and not the number of hives that is the true unit of measure. Thus, it begs the question, just how many bees are required to get the job done, and what is the cost to the bee? These commercial honey bees are no longer foraging in natural habitats of clover and wild flowers. To accomplish today's required crop pollination migration is necessary. Thus, honey bees spend week-after-week on the road, carried on large transport trucks (sometimes smaller vehicles), feeding on one single crop at a time. They essentially follow the blooming season of various commercially grown crops, traveling long distances to meet the needs of the next flowering produce. They are often undernourished and overworked ~ migration itself is stressful.

Commercial Beekeeping ~ Economic Impact

The honey bee's pollination efforts are responsible for a 3rd of all the food choices we have today; so things are not going to change any time soon. Bees alone pollinate hundreds of species of plants that have no other way to reproduce and set seed.

Photo Image 5.4: Orchard of California Almonds
Credit: ablokhin /Thinkstock

It is difficult to accurately monetize the full range of services provided by the bees, but perhaps an examination of the price tag placed on commercial beekeeping pollination services for one crop in the United States can glean some insight.

To fully understand the scope of commercial beekeeping and its contribution to the economy let's examine the farming of almonds in the United States. To date, California is responsible for providing 80 percent of the global almond demand (Almond Board of California, 2015). In fact, the industry shipped 1.81 billion pounds worldwide, which accounted for 97% of California's total production. Export shipments were destined for over 90 countries, and the top three export markets were Spain, India, and Germany. In 2013, almonds were worth approximately $4.2 billion in export value; a 23% increase from 2012 (Almond Board of California, 2015). That's just one crop! How do they meet this need… honey bees, and lots of bees. Every year commercial beekeepers transport about 60% of *all* U.S. honey bees to the California almond groves during the months of February and March, when it's still winter in most other state (Driessen, 2014). Aside from the amount of water needed to

nourish this crop, what should now be crystal clear, is that this industry requires a huge amount of honey bee pollinators to get the job done ~ to ensure crop fertilization occurs.

So just how many bees do you think are required for this industry to flourish?

Photo Image 5.5: Bee Hives in the Almond Orchard
Credit: Richard Thornton/Shutterstock

This amount of crop yield would require roughly two hives' worth for every acre of almonds trees, totaling 1.7 million hives altogether. That's almost 85 percent of all available commercial hives in the United States, or, more than 80 billion bees (Gene Brandi, a California beekeeper who serves as vice president of the American Beekeeping Federation). And the advancement of beekeeping methods and procedures has ensured the management and availability of a high abundance of bees during the almond crop bloom (Free, 1993; Delaplane & Mayer, 2000). This is achieved by bringing hives to fields (See Photo Images 5.5: Orchard of California Almonds and Photo Image 5.4: Bee Hives in the Almond Orchard).

To elaborate on almonds, the following list of activities would ensue yearly in California, to guarantee the global almond demand is met. According to the Gene Brandi, Vice President of the American Beekeeping Federation and the USDA-NASS Honey Production Report (1986–2014), the following unfolds. Incidentally, this type of meticulous checklist would be applied to all mono-crops that depend on the assistance of commercial migratory beekeeping.

California Almonds

1.   Hives arrive in California Almond orchards just before the trees blossom

2.   As the trees blossom, bees forage for pollen and nectar in the orchard (See Photo Image 5.6: Honey bee on an Almond Blossom)

3.   When the bees move from tree-to-tree, they pollinate almond blossoms along the way. Each fertilized flower will grow into an almond

4.   After the almonds are pollinated, honey bees move throughout the United States, pollinating over 90 other crops while they make their honey

Photo Image 5.6: Honey bee on an Almond Blossom
Credit: janaph/Shutterstock

Fun Fact: Almonds are commercial bees' first natural food source after winter. The nutritious pollen helps hives grow stronger so that after the almond bloom, many beekeepers split hives to grow their apiaries.

It is both humbling and concerning to realize that this single tiny species is required to pollinate over a third of the world's food supply (Klein et al., 2007). As the human population grows, houses, factories, and highways will replace open fields of honey producing plants. And unwavering problems and dangers confront the existence of beekeeping as agricultural and land-use practices threaten their survival (Neumann & Carreck, 2010). This combined dependence and risk creates an urgency to safeguard the honey bee and heed its challenges. This issue will be further explored in Chapter 6.

Hobby or Backyard Beekeepers

The forage sources for honey bees are an important consideration for all beekeepers. In order to determine where to locate hives for maximum honey production and brood growth, one must consider the off-season. If there is no honey flow bees may have to be fed. This would not be a consideration for bees used in commercial beekeeping because they are usually fed in holding yards. If you recall, nectar contains sugars, the bee's primary source of energy required for strong wing muscles, which are needed to forage and heat the colonies during the winter (Bujok et al., 2002; Winston, 1987). On the other hand, pollen provides the protein and trace minerals that are mostly fed to the brood (after it is turned into beebread), in order to continually replenish the hive since bees loss is the normal occurrence in the life cycle and activity of a bee colony. So what food sources, and when they are available are key considerations.

According to British Beekeepers Association, it is possible for bees to fly as far as 8 kilometers (5 miles) for food; however a bee's foraging area should not extend beyond for 2-3 km (2 miles). Foraging at extreme distances wears out the wings of individual bees, reduces the worker's life expectancy and therefore the efficiency of the colony. The minimum temperature for active honeybee foraging is approximately 55 °F (13 °C). Full foraging activity is not achieved until the temperature rises to 66 °F (19 °C). But as always, some variation can occur among hives and climates. Various species of plants, accessible in large quantities that bloom throughout the three main foraging seasons should be considered.

One must also recognize that a colony contains thousands of bees who forage and carries back to the hive only very small amount of honey-making material. Any honey plants must not only produce quantities of nectar but it must also exist in large mass to provide the necessary bulk of nectar. Relatively few flowers fulfill those two conditions, although a great many serve to supply the bees with moderate amounts of nectar and thus help to tide them over during lean summer weeks. Plus, don't forget weeds; or perhaps it is time to reconsider our definition of weeds and the positive contribution they make. The dandelion ~ cursed by lawn worshippers, and loved by weed killing companies is in fact a humble source of food for honey bees. Dandelions provide a huge amount of early pollen and at a time when the bees need it most. Without pollen brood rearing in the hive would have to cease, so it is quite as important that the bees have access, so as to kick off the life-cycle of the honey bee hive.

With the variety of flowers, shrubs and trees available in today's garden centers, beginner gardeners and bee enthusiasts may become overwhelmed as to what plants and flowers they should plant to provide food for foraging bees. To succeed it is important to appreciate that plants suitable for bee foraging must be planted in high numbers before any noticeable results are seen in the amount of honey that is stored in the hive. And, bees have favourites flowers too.

Consider the knowledge you have gained regarding the anatomy of the honey bee. You can now appreciate that it will not benefit bees if you plants beautiful red geraniums and scattered them throughout the garden. Bees cannot see red. On the other hand, bees are attracted to blue, white, yellow, and purple coloured flowers. Apart from colour choice, consider the plants bloom period. A plant's pollen and nectar source depends not just on the timing but the length. Other considerations include individual plant needs. Points to consider; a plants ability to grow depends on what part of the world you live in, the quality and type of soil, the soil texture, and the range of daily temperature and precipitation. There are plenty of local experts in keen to help gardeners make informed decisions, and their knowledge will generally extend to what plant choices you might want to consider attracting and feed honey bees and all insect and bird pollinators.

 ***Don`t forget water***. It's recommended to keep a small basin of fresh water in your garden or backyard, as bees actually do get thirsty...and so do birds and other insects.

However, if your goal is to have a hive to nurture the world around you, Randy Oliver, author of ScientificBeekeeping.com, provides a set of four general rules for beekeeping to provide a positive experience for your hive ~ and you. Chart 5.1 provides an overview of his key themes.

Chart 5.1: Rules for Successful Beekeeping		
Rule		
1	Bees Need Flowers	• Keep bees where lots of flowers bloom • Consider the main months when bees are active and foraging in your community, which is generally, spring ~ summer ~ fall • If a dearth of supply occurs from time-to-time, provide a sugar syrup and/or pollen supplement o This is not cheating, its good bee **husbandry**
2	Provide a Sunny Warm Hive	• Keep bees in tight boxes with good sun exposure • Make sure there are always combs of honey available as fuel • Have a warm dry cavity in which to cluster and raise brood • Full-sun colonies are more amendable to being worked, and sting far less than those in the shade • Chilling stresses bees and shortens their lifespan and resistance to disease
3	Suppress Parasites	• Use mite-resistant bee stock • Monitor mite levels and use "natural treatments" if necessary • See Chapter 6's Topic: Major Threats, Pests and Pathogens Threatening the Honey Bees
4	Avoid Toxins	• Do not use synthetic miticides, and avoid pesticide exposure • *Rotate out old combs*
Source: Randy Oliver, author of ScientificBeekeeping.com		

Plants You Should Not Grow for Beekeeping

Regardless of where you live there are certain plants that are not good for honey making because some plants produced poisonous honey that can cause severe illness resulting in abdominal pains, nausea, headaches and even vomiting. Plants such as rhododendrons and azaleas contain a glucoside of **andromedotoxin**. Strangely, plants that are known to be poisonous to humans to eat are perfectly safe for nectar collection and honey making. One such plant is hemlock (conium maculatum). All parts of this plant contain poison alkaloids. Paralysis of the respiratory system is the usual cause of death. Visually it is a flowering plant with carrot like roots that can grow up to ten feet tall, and it is not related to the eastern hemlock coniferous tree.

Fun Fact: Socrates, the eminent Greek philosopher, represents one of the most famous cases of hemlock poisoning (See Photo Image 5.7: Socrates Drinking the Conium). In 399 BC, the 70-year-old was found guilty of **heresy** in a trial in Athens. Heresy is described as expressing an opinion that was profoundly at odds with what was generally accepted at the time he lived. It was believed that he had been corrupting the youth of Athens by leading them away from the gods (in the eyes of the law, at least). His sentence was death by the hemlock plant, which he was forced to drink. Socrates drank, and then walked around until he noticed his legs were heavy. And as in the case of all who have suffered this fatal blow ~ death by hemlock poisoning renders a victim unable to move but they are aware of what is happening as the mind is unaffected until death is forthcoming.

Photo Image 5.7: Socrates Drinking the Conium
Engraved by unknown engraver and published 1880. Greece and Rome
Credit: GeorgiosArt/Thinkstock

Beekeeping Equipment

Bee Hives

We are now at the point in our chapter when we examine the nuts and bolts; beekeeping equipment. Bee hives can be purchased with bees in them or the bees may be purchased separately. The best time to buy bees is in the spring when you can be guaranteed the arrival of a viable hive headed by a good egg laying queen. Nuclei colonies (nucs) with three or four frames of bees, brood and honey can also be purchased. If you are excited to get started, January is not too early to make arrangements for the bees to arrive in April or May.

The following photo images are samples of hive equipment based on the Langstroth design. Notice the vertical modular bee hive that allows frames to be stacked. Today, the actual dimensions of the so-called Langstroth frames differ by region or manufacturer, yet the same design advantage exist.

The bees build honeycomb into frames, which can be moved and removed with ease. The frames are designed to prevent bees from attaching honeycombs (8mm bee space), where they might otherwise connect adjacent frames or attach to the hive's outer wall. These movable frames ensure beehive management.

Photo Image 5.8: Honeycomb Foundation Beehive Wax Frame
● Observe the frames of this brood box. The frame that has been removed to provides a glimpse at the foundation from which the bees will build their brood cells and or honeycomb
Credit: Bake

Hive Box and Hive Super

Hive bodies and hive supers are four-sided boxes with standardized inside dimensions. There are generally four different sizes. Outside box dimensions vary depending on the type of material used. Polystyrene boxes have much larger outside measurements than boxes made out of wood. Deep and medium hive bodies are provided to serve as the **brood chamber**. It is here, where the queen lays eggs and the nurse bees care for the larvae and rear the young. Bees also store honey and pollen for short-term and winter use in the brood box. Photo Image 5.8; Bee Hive illustrates a 9-5/8" deep brood box. This photo image also illustrates a shallow 7 inch honey super, used for the bee's honey stores, and it provides an easy harvest for beekeepers since it can be separated from the brood box.

To prevent the queen from laying eggs in this honey super a queen excluder is placed between the brood box and the supers (See Photo Images 5.10: Queen Excluder and 5.8; Bee Hive). It is designed to be just the right size to allow the smaller workers to travel in and out, but prevent the larger queen from moving into the honey super to lay her eggs. Depending on how many brood boxes are used, the excluder can be placed between the brood boxes and honey supers.

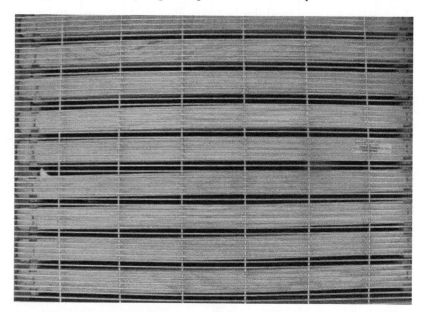

Photo Image 5.10: Queen Excluder
Credit: Bake

The hive's outer cover and inner cover are shown in Photo Image 5.8: Bee Hive. The outer cover is wooden (could also be purchased in a polystyrene material) and it fits on the top of the hive about an inch or so down over the top super (called a telescoping cover). The cover protects the inner cover.

The inner cover provides a barrier between the telescoping cover and the bees. It prevents the bees from gluing the top cover to the top bars of the super. When an inner cover is used, the top is more easily removed from the hive. Notches in the frame of the solid inner cover and telescoping cover can serve as an upper entrance for the bees. A communication hole in the middle allows bees to reach emergency food if placed above by the beekeeper. The entire box sits, or rests on a bottom board; which essentially is the floor of the beehive (See Photo Image 5.8: Honey Bee Hive). It consists of several rails that serve as a frame around a solid piece of wood, protects the hive from damp ground.

Hive Cover

**7 inch
10 frame
Honey Super**

**Queen
Excluder**

**Brood box
9-5/8" deep
10 frame**

Bottom Board

Photo Image 5.8: Honey Bee Hive
Langstroth Design Hive
Credit: Bake

Bees

The best time to buy bees is in the spring when you can ensure that you receive a viable hive headed by a good laying (mated) queen. Nuclei colonies (nucs) with three or four frames of bees, brood and honey can also be purchased. It is best to check with local beekeepers to make the best individual choice.

Honey and Comb cut off the Frame

Smoking Bees

A smoker (See Photo Image 5.11: Smoker) is required equipment when either examining the hive, and or harvesting the honey. In fact it might be more appropriate to say it is the *most* essential beekeeping tool. It bellows out thick, cool smoke from a fire chamber. The smoke makes the bees easier to handle during inspections. It will

be extremely helpful as you work with your hive to have a stand or a structure nearby to place the smoker on because it will continue to bellow out smoke as you handle the individual frames.

Photo Image 5.11: Smoker
⬡ All fired up and ready to inspect the hive and its brood. Notice the thick white bellowing smoke.
Credit: Bake

Why use the smoker? Smoke is used to change the bees' behaviour, as it prevents them from becoming defensive during inspection or when harvesting honey. Langstroth wrote in 1860, "By the use of a little smoke from decayed wood, the largest and most fiery colony may at once be brought into complete subjections. As soon as the smoke is blown among them, they retreat from before it, raising a subdued or terrified note, and seeing to imagine that their home is to be taken from them, they cram their honey-bags to their utmost capacity" (p.27). Langstroth awareness was undeniably accurate, however bee knowledge has advanced and today's justification for this bee behaviour stems from the fact that the smoke masks the alarm pheromone released from the bee's Nasonov gland, which is located at the end of the worker's abdomen (Seeley, 2010). This pheromone would generally be released by workers when the hive is opened, triggering a defense action on the part of the colony. The introduction of smoke also interferes with their ability to communicate. Refer to Chapter 3, Illustration 3.2: Anatomy of the Honey Bee, to locate the Nasonov gland.

Honey Extracting

Harvesting the honey crop involves several steps, and specific equipment is required. The first step is to separate the combs of honey from the bees (pulling the honey). This can be as simple as using a bee brush to sweep the bees from each frame. With just a few hives a bee brush is adequate and inexpensive.

Honey Extractors

Once the hive super frames are full the extraction begins. Honey extractors have been around for years and it was first invented by Major Franz Elder von Hruschka in 1864/1865. He was born in Vienna and resided near Venice (Mangum, 2016).   As for the spark of his insight that directed him to the centrifugal principle (spinning); separating the comb and liquid honey, one story has circulated for eras, although its authenticity lay in doubt. Mangum (2016) reported that in 1865, Major Hruschka…gave his small son a piece of honeycomb on a plate. Placing the honey in a basket, the boy swung the basket around his head as children commonly do when carrying any kind of object. When Hruschka saw the honey was thrown from the comb by the motion, the idea of the extractor was born. Such is the story commonly told, although historians question the facts. They say the extractor was born of a long search for a way to remove the honey. Before the honey extractor became well known the traditional way to buy honey was in with the comb.

Photo Image: 5.12: Old Wooden Honey Extractor
Credit: dja65/Thinkstock

Today, extractors range in size from two-frame, hand-powered devices (See Photo Image 5.13: Hand-powered Honey Extractor), to motor-driven machines that can simultaneously handle 100 or more frames (See Photo Image 5.14: Midsection of Senior Beekeeper Operating Honey Extraction plant in Factory). Before the honey can be released an additional device will be needed to remove the wax cappings from the honey comb. An electrically heated knife is commonly used.

Photo Image 5.13: Hand-powered Honey Extractor
Credit: mady70/Thinkstock

After the honey is extracted the next phase involves straining the honey. Cheesecloth or a nylon cloth can work. Once complete the honey should then be stored in a warm place in a tall tank or container to allow the fine impurities to rise to the top. At this point it helps to have a proper tank with an outlet at the bottom so that the clean, warm honey can be drawn from the bottom directly into the honey containers.

Photo Image 5.14: Midsection of Senior Beekeeper Operating Honey Extraction plant in Factory
⬡ Notice the bee glue on top of the frames
Credit: Tyler Olson/Shutterstock

Beekeeping Cloths

Bees tend to attack the face of mammals, including human and this innate ability developed to protect the hive against the threat of bears. A jacket and hat with a veil is an essential tool for beekeepers. If one is nervous around bees, they may breathe more heavily, which can lead to stings. Many experienced beekeepers do not wear any gear, and have become so comfortable around their bees; they can behave calmly and not get stung. Yet, it is recommended using of at least a hat/veil combinations. Gloves and white, loose clothing is also suggested.

Beekeeping Clothing Checklist

1. Beekeeping Jacket Suit or Dress Smock
   - Invest in professional quality
2. Hat-Veil; they are sold together
3. Beekeeping Protective Gloves
   - It is advisable to become comfortable with your bare hands, because it allows you to manipulate, grab and work with the hive more precisely.
     - This is the moment when the smoker becomes essential.
4. Shoes, socks
   - If not wearing an entire suit, make sure the socks are tucked into the pants.

Note: If you plan to inspire the beekeeper in others, invest in extra equipment to safely share the experience!

Conclusion

Beekeeping has evolved to become an enormous business. Few of us however will work in or own one of these large pollination companies or farms. In fact, in the United States, the vast majority (nearly 96 percent) of the 2.2 million farms are family owned and operated (Dunckel, 2013). But hopefully this chapter has sweetened the idea that perhaps a hive perfectly placed on your property or in a community garden will provide a safe home for a colony of bees to thrive, while pollinating our much desired and needed plants, shrubs, and trees.

Photo Image 5.15: Kew Gardens, London, England
- London's largest UNESCO World Heritage site offering unique landscapes and iconic architecture from every stage of the Garden's history
- Note the beehives. The smaller units are solitary beehives; providing homes for bumble bees.
- The tall white unit is a William Broughton Carr (WBC) design, and second from the left is a Langstroth Hive

Credit: Girdler, 2016

CHAPTER REVIEW QUESTIONS

1. In Canada approximately how many species of trees are there?
   a. 80
   b. 180
   c. 380
   d. 580

2. Berries are the largest honey bee pollinated crop in The United States.
   a. True
   b. False

3. The total value of honey produced in Canada totals over $1 billion dollars.
   a. False
   b. True

4. How does Canada's forests area rate in terms of size compared to other countries in the world?
   a. It is the largest in the world
   b. It is the second-largest in the world
   c. It is the third-largest in the world
   d. It is the fourth-largest in the world

5. Beekeeping protective gloves are the most important piece of clothing to use when keeping bees?
   a. True
   b. False

6. Which country was Canada's top honey export destination?
   a. China
   b. Greece
   c. Japan
   d. United States

7. Who is credited with creating the first system of Queen Rearing?
   a. Henry Alley
   b. Gilbert M. Doolittle
   c. L.L. Langstroth
   d. Major Hruschka

8. Who invented the honey extractor?
   a. Henry Alley
   b. Gilbert M. Doolittle
   c. L.L. Langstroth
   d. Major Hruschka

9. Greek philosopher Socrates died of a bee sting?
   a. True
   b. False

10. Which State grows the pollinated crop that provides 80 percent of the global demand?
    a. Oregon
    b. Michigan
    c. Florida
    d. California

ACTIVITIES

To enhance your understanding and nurture your curiosities check out the following:

I.   The Canadian Forestry website
  • http://canadianforestry.com/wp/national-forest-week/

II. Check out the Statistical Overview of the Canadian Honey and Bee Industry 2013-2014
  • http://www.agr.gc.ca/resources/prod/doc/pdf/1453219857143-eng.pdf

KEY TERMS

Andromedotoxin
  • A toxic poisonous compound found in various plants of the heath family (Ericaceae) that lowers the blood pressure of animals when taken in small doses

Cottage industry
  • A business that involves people producing things at home

Gilbert M. Doolittle
  • In 1889: Considered father of Commercial queen rearing

Gross income/ Net income
  • Refers to the total amount before anything is deducted
  • The amount remaining after certain adjustments have been made for debts, deductions or expenses

Henry Alley
  • In 1861; concentrated on rearing queen bees; Developed the Alley method of Queen-Rearing

Husbandry
  • The care, cultivation, and breeding of crops and animals

Monocropping
  • Agricultural practice of a one-crop economy, where income relies solely on the production and sale of one agricultural crop

Chapter 5: Review and Study Notes

Chapter 5: Review and Study Notes

Chapter 6
Social Justice and Advocacy ~ *Bee*lieve

"Compassion is the radicalism of our time."

~ Dalai Lama XIV ~

Chapter Objectives

After reading this chapter you should be able to:

1. Value the influence Rachel Carson's advocacy and her book the *Silent Spring* had on the environmental movement
2. Explain the history of DDT, its initial use and the impact on society
3. Classify and describe the Major Threats, Pests and Pathogens Threatening the Honey Bee
4. Discuss Colony Collapse Disorder
5. Identify Key Comrades in Compassion and how they have accomplished to Protect our Earth
6. Decide how you might become a bee advocate

Introduction

Chances are you have heard the expression "social movements". Today it is virtually impossible to not turn on our televisions or computers without being informed of an act of protest somewhere in the world. This is not a new phenomenon, countless historical and present day examples exist. For instance, the animal rights movement, civil rights and women's movement, and more recently, black lives matter. Various mediums have also bound people together; button and tee-shirt wearing, sit-ins and sip-ins, holding signs and marching, and chants to name only a few. The emotional levels of protests have also fluctuated; from the calm and measured, to the angry and violent (Bake, 2013; Koopmans, 1993; Michel, 1949; Snot wet al., 1980). "The pen is mightier than the sword", approach has been embraced through poetry and music, letters to the editor, and academic publishing. And in recent years social media has provided a larger platform that has supported inspiring new and creative alternatives. Movements occur to express dissatisfaction with the status quo, and present diverging views often fueled by new important facts, innovative and creative ideas and solutions.

Movements have also problemize the ways in which we live our lives, and sometimes call for urgent changes in our thoughts and habits.

Many if not most of you have heard the name David Suzuki… and what idea is induced? Chances are a variety of descriptions arise, yet a universal theme might be to advocate for and act in the best interests to preserved planet Earth's fragile ecosystem. The David Suzuki Foundation specifically states we have a mission to protect the diversity of nature and our quality of life, now and for the future. Moreover, "Our vision is that within a generation, Canadians act on the understanding that we are all interconnected and interdependent with nature". It is with this ethos in mind that we enter the last chapter of our Exploration of the Life and Times of the Honey Bee, and ask ourselves how we might answer the question … *To Bee or Not to Bee*?

DDT ~ Rachel Louise Carson's Formidable Foe

Even before Dr. Suzuki began his weekly television children's show *Suzuki on Science* in 1970, or when he co-founded the David Suzuki Foundation in 1990, or when a global environmental movement was launched by Green Peace in Vancouver, British Columbia in 1971, there was Rachel Louise Carson. Who you might ask? Some might state with great conviction that you are about to be introduced to a hero; a person of highest integrity and vision, because Carson spoke and wrote truth even when the people she was challenging were those who were themselves powerful. But to allow you the opportunity to make an informed decision we will first explore and evaluate the reasons behind DDT's conception and its historical impact.

DDT (dichloro-diphenyl-trichloroethane) was conceived out of the urgent need to control typhus. This disease has existed throughout human history, and was transferred to humans usually by exposure to vectors such as fleas or lice. Canada also documented one of its tragic historical experiences. For instance, in Kingston, Ontario, a Historical Plaque was erected that reads, The Typhus Epidemic of 1847 (Ontario's Historical Plaques). It commemorated the worst outbreak that occurred in 1847, when approximately 16,000 of the 90,000 Irish emigrants who had embarked for

Canada died of typhus at sea. And despite the efforts of local religious and charitable organizations to help the ill upon their arrival, many more would die (See ACTIVITY Section).

The typhus epidemic appeared again in Europe between 1914 and 1918 (WW1), and it would be responsible for the death of approximately 20–30 million people. Following World War I, during the Russian Civil War (1917 – 1922), typhus killed an additional three million people, and most of those causalities were civilians. These unrelenting public health concerns could not be ignored. You can perhaps now appreciate why, in 1939 a game changer of sorts was discovered that would eliminate typhus's transmission ~ **DDT**. DDT was first synthesized in 1874, but in 1939, its insecticidal properties were discovered when Swiss chemist Paul Hermann Müller realized its effectiveness to control diseases (NobelPrize.org). DDT was also praised for its colourless, tasteless, and virtually odourless qualities. Later in 1948, Dr. Müller would receive the Nobel Prize in Physiology or Medicine for his discovery (Conniff, 2015; Fletcher, 2010; NobelPrize.org).

Armed with this new pesticide and determiend to prevent the numerous fatalities that had occurred during WW1, DDT de-lousing stations were established for troops on the Western front and in the South Pacific throughout WW2 (1940-1945). It was also sprayed aerially to control the insect vectors resspossible for malaria, dengue fever, and typhus (See Photo Image 6.1). As a consequence, DDT's use contributed to the near elimination of these diseases in many parts of Europe, and it would be celebrated and valued for its life saving capability (Dunlap, 2014). And since DDT killed the lice on millions of refugees, even larger epidemics in post-war Europe were prevented. In 1949,The World Health Organization claimed that by applying this pesticide 25 million lives were saved.

To add to the fervor of DDT's importance and celebrity were two prevailing post-WW2 American philosophies. First, was the government's promise to safeguard the health and safety of its citizens (Brooks, 1972; Lear, 1997). Secondly, there was a prevailing belief that scientists were infallible, thus so too were their endorsement s that chemical pesticides were considered society's friend. Additionally, regulating the use of insecticides was the responsibility of the Department of Agriculture, which also happened to be one of DDT's greatest beneficiaries.

In America between 1945 and 1970, to help control insects that threatened agricultural crops, DDT was made available as a crop insecticide (Larson, 2007). It also became common in cities across

North America to conduct aerial pesticide spray-overs, aiming for farm lands, streams and lakes, beaches, and city homes, streets, and parks. In time large quantities of DDT were released into the air, on the soil, and in the water.

DDT was also relatively inexpensive to manufacture and so effective that it became an everyday household product. DDT was sprayed in gardens, homes and yes, even in their mattresses (Please see Photo Image 6.1: DDT Spraying Gun). The Sherwin Williams Company even began marketing DDT in a paintable form in the mid 1940's under the trade name Pestroy.

Photo Image 6.1: DDT Spraying Gun
Credit: Thinkstock/Hemera Technologies

Those who swallowed large amounts of DDT, or who were exposed to it while working would become excitable. Some individuals would even have tremors and seizures. Other symptoms included; sweating, headache, nausea, vomiting, and dizziness and fatigue (Casida and Quistad, 1998). Similar symptoms would occur by breathing DDT air bound particles. Once exposure stopped the effects on the nervous system went away. To further examine this time in history please check out the ACTIVITY section to watch the video; The American experience: Rachel Carson (Casida & Quistad, 1998; Longnecker, 1997).

What is vital to appreciate, is that before Rachel Carson published her book, words and phrases such as, environmental activism, think green, and *Reduce, Reuse, Recycle*, didn't exist, and there was no such thing as an Environmental Protection Agency. Carson's *Silent Spring* would call out the horrid little fact that DDT produced neurological and fertility problems in humans, and accumulated up the food chain in wildlife, poisoning birds (Fletcher, 2010).

Rachel Louise Carson
The Book that Inspired the Environmental Movement

Rachel Carson was born in 1907 and died in 1964. She was an American marine biologist who began her career working for the U.S. Bureau of Fisheries as an aquatic biologist. She became a nature writer and in 1941 when she published her first book, *Under the Sea Wind: A Naturalist's Picture of Ocean Life*. In the 1951 she wrote *The Sea Around Us,* which won her a U.S. National Book Award in 1952. In the late 1950s, she became interested in conservation; particularly the problems that she believed were caused by synthetic pesticides. The outcome of her work would lead to her 1962 publication, *Silent Spring* (Brooks, 1972; Lear, 1997).

Carson's book, ideology and facts were met with angry opposition as they were honest, straightforward, diverging from the status quo, and thus unwelcomed. At the time of its release the New York Times wrote "*Silent Spring* is now a noisy summer" (Carson, 1962, p.xi). The contents within created a watershed moment, generating the sale of more than 500,000 copies in 24 countries, and it spent almost eight months, a total of thirty-one weeks on the New York Times best-seller list. What set off the fire storm; *pesticides*. In her book Carson wrote,

> For the first time in the history of the world, every human being is now subjected to contact with dangerous chemicals, from the moment of conception until death. In the less than two decades of their use, the synthetic pesticides have been so thoroughly distributed throughout the **animate** an **inanimate** world that they occur virtually everywhere. They have been recovered from most of the major river systems and even from streams of the groundwater flowing unseen through the earth. Residues of these chemical linger in soil to which they have been applied a dozen years before… They occur in mother's milk and probably in the tissue of the unborn child. (1962, pgs.15-16)

As one would imagine, fierce pushback also ensued from the very wealthy and influential chemical companies, particularly from DuPont, who was the key manufacturer of DDT, and the Velsicol Chemical Company; the exclusive manufacture of chlordane and heptachlor (Brooks, 1972; Lear, 1997). The pesticide industry and many others attacked Carson's findings, calling them hysterical. In the wake of this storm, President Kennedy convened a committee to assess Carson's evidence, and in time the committee's review would vindicate her findings (Brooks, 1972; Lear, 1997).

Amid the angry disparaging backlash, an important consequence arose. Carson's book set off a national debate on the use of chemical pesticides, the responsibility of science, and the limits of technological progress. When she died just two years after her publication, at the young age of 56, she set into motion the course of events that would eventually result in a ban on the domestic production of DDT (Brooks, 1972; Lear, 1997). Later in 1970, a swelling environmental movement would fuel the creation of the U.S. Environmental Protection Agency, (the USEPA). The agency mission was to protect human health and the environment by writing and enforcing regulations, and to ensure these laws were passed by the United States Congress (Brooks, 1972; Lear, 1997).

Since Rachel Carson's death her work and advocacy have been honoured by many. Groups ranging from government institutions to environmental and conservation organizations to scholarly societies have all celebrated her life and work. Carson is a frequent namesake for prizes awarded by philanthropic, educational and scholarly institutions. In 1994, an edition of Silent Spring was published with a new introduction penned by Vice President Al Gore.

Our modern day social media would also step up, and in 2014, for Carson's 107th birthday, Google created a Rachel Carson Google Doodle. Yet, perhaps the most meaningful, was in 1980, when Carson was posthumously awarded the Presidential Medal of Freedom, the highest civilian honour in the United State (Brooks, 1972; Lear, 1997). And in the following year,1981, a Great Americans postage stamp honoured her, with a 17¢ stamp (See Imagine: 6.2 Great Americans series~ Rachel Carson).

Image: 6.1; The Great Americans series honours Rachel Carson
USA - CIRCA 1981: A stamp printed in USA shows portrait of Rachel Carson (1907-1964)
Credit: Solodov Aleksey/Shutterstock

More recently, in 2011, Time Magazine would recognize DDT as one of The 50 Worst Inventions (Fletcher, 2010).

Despite the furry and criticism hurled against her, during her life time Rachel Carson remained quietly determined. Her authentic motivation was driven from a passion for science, and a lifelong interest in the history of the earth. A vital outcome intrinsic to all movement is to have its goal realized. "Caron's writings initiated a transformation into relationship between human and the natural world, and stirred an awakening of public environmental consciousness" (Carson, 1962, xi).

After Rachel Carson Sounded the Alarm

Human health concerns would continue to grow due to the continuing accumulation of the **water-insoluble** nature of DDT and its impact on the environment. In time International action was taken and it was banned in the United States and in most of the world by 1972. The registered use of DDT was suspended in Canada in 1985, and the use of existing stocks was only permitted until the end of 1990. Even more specifically, DDT is now prohibited under the Canada–Ontario Agreement Respecting the Great Lakes Basin Ecosystem (COA). The purpose of the COA is, "To restore, protect and conserve the Great Lakes Basin Ecosystem in order to assist in achieving the vision of a healthy, prosperous and sustainable Basin Ecosystem for present and future generations" (Environment Canada and the

Great Lakes

Can you name all the Lakes?

Ontario Ministry of the Environment, 2011). DDT was also banned worldwide for agricultural uses at the 2001 Stockholm Convention on Persistent Organic Pollutants (Pesticide action network, 2017). The original Canadian Environmental Protection Act (CEPA) was enacted in 1988.

Canadian Environmental Protection Act, 1999

- Is one of the most significant environmental laws in Canada governing the assessment and management of chemical substances
- The Act`s purpose is to protect the environment, and the health and well-being of Canadians
- A major part of the Act is to sustainably prevent pollution and address the potentially dangerous chemical substances to which we might be exposed

History

- The original *Canadian Environmental Protection Act* (CEPA) was enacted in 1988
- It provided a systematic approach to assess and manage chemical substances in the environment that were not addressed under existing programs
- After an examination in the 1990s, it was replaced with the current legislation (CEPA; 1999) that provides new powers for health and environmental protection
- It was introduced as *Bill C-32* on March 12, 1998, and received Royal Assent on September 14, 1999
- The new Act came into force on March 31, 2000
- Together, the Ministers of Environment and Health are responsible for CEPA`s enforcement

---

Major Threats, Pests and Pathogens Threatening the Honey Bees

Honey bees are critical pollinators of many important agricultural crops and they currently face multiple stressors (Klein et al., 2007; Bromenshenk et al., 2010; Potts et al., 2010; Calderone, 2012). As human population increases, houses, factories, and highways replace open fields of honey and pollen plants. Pests, parasites and pathogens are also significant concerns. Some diseases are worse than others, and many of them have been an on-going challenge faced by beekeepers in much of the world (Tew, 2015). The most established diseases are; American Foulbrood, varroa mites, tracheal mites, and wax moths (See Chart 6.1; Overview of Honey Bee Diseases).To begin the discussion on the threats of the honey bee, an examination of the Colony Collapse Disorder (CCD) is required.

Colony Collapse Disorder

Colony Collapse Disorder (CCD) is the biggest threat to hives. A beekeeper may check the hive one day and all seems fine; yet the next day may find the bees have disappeared. The bees are not lying dead at the entrance, but gone! Historically the symptoms associated with CCD have been called many names, for instance; Fall or Spring Dwindle Disease or Disappearing Disease (van Engelsdorp et al., 2006). However, a name change resulted in 2006, when CCD exploded onto the agricultural scene, when numerous beekeepers went out to their apiaries that spring and found that many of the bees in their colonies had mysteriously vanished. Nor was this a problem specific to one geographic area, because European, Canadian and apiarist world-wide observed these drastic outcomes (Winston, 2014). And the bee losses were not insignificant numbers, almost one-third of all colonies from around the planet were gone (DuPont et. al., 2007; Oldroyd, 2007). In 2014, Winston wrote, "Since 2006, CCD has not abated, posing a continuing and increasing threat to beekeeping as well as the numerous crops that rely on bees. Annual colony loses of 30 to 40 percent are now routine globally, and losses can go as high as 100 percent for some beekeepers" (2014, p. 61).

Critical to understanding the Colony Collapse Disorder crisis is the fact that it is not occurring in a vacuum. Honey bee health is affected by the diseases and pests that have long challenged beekeepers, however the practices of the agriculture industry, which is outside of beekeeping makes bee management problematic (Tew, 2015; Winston, 2014). Farms today have changed, and many grow single-crops fields which are treated with insecticides and fungicides. Even the weed killers; herbicides, have eliminated alterative foraging sources for bees. The loss of diverse vegetation has also created a serious problem that has been unfolding during the past decades (Tew, 2015; Winston, 2014).

Photo Image 6.2: Varroa destructor mite on a Honey Bee Pupa
Credit: Mirko Graul/Shutterbox

In addition to the agriculture industry's practices, is the challenge to control the pests that have longed harmed the health of bees and their colonies. For instance Varroa mites, were first introduced in the 1980, and are considered to be the number one enemy of the honey bee and beekeepers around the world (Tew, 2015; The Ontario Beekeepers Association, 2012; Winston, 2014). These external parasites feed on the blood of adult honey bees, and reproduce on honey bee pupae (See Photo Image 6.2: Varroa destructor mite on a honey bee pupa).They considerably weaken individual bees, and transfer viruses and other pathogens between bees. Mites are spread to other colonies through drifting and robbing. Moreover, their high capacity to reproduce makes dealing with mites a huge challenge for beekeepers (Tew, 2015).

In an effort to address these pests, beekeepers would find themselves on the same pesticide treadmill as the agriculture industry (Winston, 2014). Recommended antivarroa miticides were applied, but they were used with greater amounts and frequently than recommended. Predictably the bees acquired resistance and the chemical(s) lost effectiveness. Naturally, another new antivarroa would appear, and again the pattern repeated. Yet, the destructive effect of Varroa alone is not the sole explanation of Colony Collapse Disorder.

Although modern insecticides were originally thought to be safe, recent studies have suggested that many chemicals interfere with the bee's immune system increasing their susceptibility to disease (Tew, 2015; Winston, 2014). Scientists began to investigate the complex relationship between the bee's weakening immune systems, the fungal and bacterial diseases, and how they became resistant to antibiotics. They were particularly interested in the American foulbrood (AFB) because is the most serious brood disease harming honey bees. AFB is caused by a spore forming bacteria. This disease is highly contagious, and will weaken and in most cases kill an entire honey bee colony. Regrettably there is no cure for AFB, and beekeepers can only take steps to prevent an infection from establishing itself in a beekeeping operation.

As the quest to find the silver bullet to solve CCD continued, scientists furthered their investigation and began to study the impact and relationship between the antibiotics and chemicals. In time a researcher who reared worker bees became worried by the new systemic insecticides, a type of pesticide in which seeds are coated before planting. And this is where the emerging alarm regarding another pesticide began; neonicitinoids (neonics) (Winston, 2014).

The name, neonicotinoid insecticides, literally means "new nicotine-like insecticides". Like nicotine, the neonicotinoids act on certain kinds of receptors in the nerve synapse. They are much more toxic to insects, than they are to mammals, birds and other higher organisms. Initially it was believed that this form of insecticide application would be safe since it avoided aerial spraying that would potentially kill non- targeted insects they were praised for their low-toxicity. As such neonics were marketed in the agriculture sector as a way to protect crops from harmful insects. But as time and research has unearthed they are much more toxic.

Neonicotinoid are systemic, which means they are taken up through leaves or roots, and spread throughout the plant. Moreover, they cannot be washed or peeled off crops. Despite early claims, studies have now shown that these pesticides are also likely to harm "non-target organisms". Tiny amounts of neonics do make their way into nectar and pollen and harm species beyond the insects they're designed to control. They have been linked to the wild pollinator declines and honey bee die-offs. In addition, a growing body of scientific literature documents the adverse effects neonicotinoids have on the foraging and homing (communication) behaviour of bees, as well as their metabolic, immune and reproductive functions.

Photo Image 6.3: Save Our Bees
⬡ Basel, Switzerland - May 21, 2016 - 2000 people demonstrate against agrochemical corporations Monsanto, Syngenta and ChemChina
Credit: lucarista/Shutterstock

One might wonder what Rachel Carson would think about our present day problem, as we find ourselves once again demanding the same action. In 2013, The European Union restricted the use of four neonicotinoid pesticides, including clothianidin, because of the risk to bee health. (See Photo Image 6.3: Save Our Bees).

Massive bee die-offs have occurred over the past two years in Manitoba, Ontario and Quebec which have been linked to the use of neonicotinoid pesticides (Croome & Hatt, 2016). Dr. Suzuki has emphatically stated that Canada must ban neonics.

In 2016, lawyers from the Canadian Environmental Law Association and Ecojustice filed a Notice of Objection with the health minister on behalf of the David Suzuki Foundation, Sierra Club Canada, Wilderness Committee, and Équiterre. The objection concerns Health Canada's recent decision to renew the registration for clothianidin, which the groups say should be banned in Canada. This story is not yet over, but thanks to our compassionate and passionate environmental activists, the issues will not disappear, and hopefully neither will the honey bee.

Chart 6.1: Overview of Honey Bee Diseases and Pests	
American Foulbrood (AFB)	• The most serious brood disease of honey bees • Caused by a spore-forming bacteria; specific to honey bees • Highly contagious, will weaken and potentially kill a bee colony • Will also contaminate beekeeping equipment so it must be destroyed to prevent the spread • No cure ~ Beekeepers can only take steps to prevent an infection from establishing itself in a beekeeping operation
Tracheal Mites	• Internal parasites • Live and breed inside the tracheal tubes which insects use to breathe • Increased selection has improved the honey bees' natural resistance to this pest
Varroa mites	• Are external parasites • Are #1 enemy of honey bee and beekeepers globally • Feed on the blood of adult honey bees, and reproduce on honey bee pupae. They weaken bees, and transfer viruses and other pathogens between bees. Highly reproductive makes managing them a challenge
Wax Moths	• A cunning pest found in honey bee hives • Causes significant damage to stored combs • The best defense against is to keep colonies strong and healthy
Sources: Tew, 2015; The Ontario Beekeepers Association, 2012; Winston, 2014	

A Case of Mistaken Identity… *Who's in your neighbourhood?*

Although not as serious as the aforementioned content, this issue should be addressed. Too often bees are mistaken for wasp, a term used to describe both hornets and yellow jackets, and this gives them a bad reputation and it compounds the problems bees face. They are not the carnivore insects who fly around your summer BBQ looking to land. Therefore to use a famous English idiom, "a picture is worth a thousand words"; let's shine a light on those honey bee imposters. One of the key differences between wasps and hornets is that wasp colonies tend to be smaller, with fewer than 100 individuals, while hornet colonies typically have many more.

It is often difficult to tell the difference, but they are both hairless and thin-bodied. Yellowjackets also tend to have more exact black and white stripes running across their bodies than do hornets (See Photo Image 6.4: A number of Wasps on a Comb). Yellowjackets also nest underground in areas that have been hollowed out by rodents or other animals. Hornets, prefer to stay above ground,

nesting in trees, sheds, shrubs and perhaps under eaves of homes. They both build their nests out of wood materials ground up into paper. (See Photo 6.5: Wasp on comb; its nest). Notice how drastically different its living quarters is compared to the honey bee. But be warned, both the wasp and hornet will vigorously defend its comb.

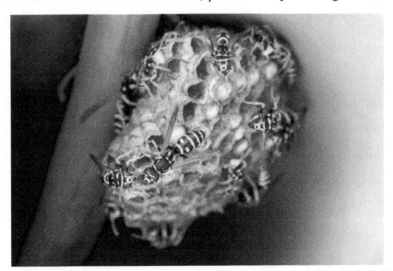

Photo Image 6.4: A number of Wasps on Comb
Credit: diatrezor/ Thinkstock
Photo Image 6.5: One Hornet emerging
Credit: SKatzenberger/Thinkstock

Comrades in Compassion

Planet Earth Advocates
Let's add your name!

> *"We stand at a critical moment in Earth's history, a time when humanity must choose its future.*
> *As the world becomes increasingly interdependent and fragile, the future at once holds great peril and great promise."*
>
> **~ The Earth Charter ~**

Let's begin the last section of our textbook with a moment of self-reflection. One goal of this academic journey was to provide you with an overview of vital information to nurture your ability to glean a couple important truths. Now that you have been introduced to the honey bee I would imagine you have been unexpectedly swept off your feet by the vital role bees play in nourishing human life and the environmental ecosystem. You have also studied many challenges that collectively contribute to the bee's declining global populations. Thus, the question must be asked... has this knowledge cultivated *your* need to act? If the answer is yes, how could you get involved?

Could you plant a bee friendly garden; bees need food. Happily, what bees need is what gardeners like too ~ a variety of plants that bloom at different times throughout the year. Hostas and sunflowers are favourites, and so too are dandelions; *the honey bee's field of dreams.* So why not embrace those bright yellow flowers that arrive every spring in our meadows, parks and lawns? Or if time and space are an issue, just grow a favourite flower in a decorative container. How about a tree? Now that you can identify the endless gifts trees provide to our earth why not dig in and plant. Bees love maples and lindens. Or, could you build or buy bees a home? These progressive actions can also extend to and support other pollinators, and it is easy to do. By putting out nests of cardboard tubes or wooden bee boxes in a patch of bare earth, in a dry sunny spot, you can attract bumblebees and ground-nesters such as digger bees and sweat bees. Remember many other pollinators suffer from diseases and a lack of diverse vegetation.

Further to the abovementioned, a different form of advocacy could occur. Might you forage for like-minded friends and start a letter writing campaign, a blog or demonstration? To help facilitate the possibilities available to you, the last section of this text is devoted to honouring Comrades in Compassion. The following are just a few examples of some of the groups, people, and actions that have been taken to protect the Earth. Perhaps they will stimulate your creativity and compassion. Here are a few; World Wildlife Fund, The United Nations Earth Charter, Green Peace, Arbour Day, and our last invitee might inspire you to take off our shoes and wiggling your toes in the soil and celebrate Earth Day.

World Wildlife Fund

World Wildlife Fund is the oldest organization that is presented in this text. Conceived in April, 1961, for the past 55₊ years, the World Wildlife Fund (WWF) has been protecting the future of nature. When it was first conceived it set up its headquarters in Morges, Switzerland. At this time, H.R.H. Prince Bernhard of the Netherlands became the organization's first president. Also in 1961, H.R.H. Prince Philip, the Duke of Edinburgh (The husband of Queen Elizabeth), became president of the British National Appeal, the first national organization in the World Wildlife Fund family. Perhaps it was the love of bees fostered by Prince Albert and Queen Victoria that nurtured future Royals descendants to act compassionately and decisively. Since these early days the WWF now works in 100 countries involving millions of members globally. WWF's values its unique way of working, by combining global reach with a foundation in science and action at every level from local to global to ensure the delivery of innovative solutions that meet the needs of both people and nature (WWF's website).

Over the decades the WWF's focus has also evolved from not only saving species and landscapes, to addressing the larger global threats and forces that impact them. Their existing strategy places people at the center, and arranges their work into six main areas: forests, marine, freshwater, wildlife, food and climate. By connecting these six areas in an united approach they leverage their assets and direct all the WWF's resources to protecting vulnerable places, species and communities worldwide (WWF's website).

The United Nations Earth Charter

The Earth Charter is an ethical framework for building a just, sustainable, and peaceful global society in the 21st century. The Charter was finalized as a people's charter on June 29, 2000. It seeks to inspire in all people a new sense of global interdependence and shared responsibility for the well-being of the whole human family, the greater community of life, and future generations. It is a vision of hope and a call to action (http://earthcharter.org/discover/what-is-the-earth-charter/). The document is divided into 4 sections (called pillars), which have sixteen main principles containing sixty-one supporting principles. The document opens with a preamble and ends with a conclusion entitled "The Way Forward".

UN Earth Charter's Four Pillars of Sustainability

- Respect & Care for The Community of Life
- Social & Economic Justice
- Democracy, Nonviolence, & Peace
- Ecological Integrity

The idea of the Earth Charter originated in 1987, by Maurice Strong and Mikhail Gorbachev when they were members of The Club of Rome, conceived when the United Nations World Commission on Environment and Development called for a new charter to guide the transition to sustainable development. Maurice Strong was a Canadian oil and mineral businessman, and in the early 1970s he was Secretary General of the United Nations Conference on the Human Environment. Later Strong became the first executive director of the United Nations Environment Programme. He returned to Canada to become Chief Executive Officer of Petro-Canada from 1976 to 1978. In 1986, he served as a commissioner of the World Commission on Environment and Development, and was recognized as a leader in the international environmental movement.

The Earth Charter has been formally endorsed by organizations representing millions of people, some examples include; The United Nations Educational, Scientific and Cultural Organization

(UNESCO), over 250 universities around the world, various religious groups from a wide range of religions, and dozens of youth organizations to name only a few.

Greenpeace ~ *The Don't Make a Wave Group*

Greenpeace first began as The Don't Make a Wave group. It was an anti-nuclear organization formed in 1970, in Vancouver, British Columbia, Canada to protest and attempt to halt the underground nuclear testing by the United States in the National Wildlife refuge at Amchitka in the Aleutian Islands of Alaska (Watson, 1981). Later in 1971, they changed their name to Greenpeace; a global environmental organization (See Photo Image 6.6: Greenpeace). Today it is has grown to include dedicated activists from more than 50 countries. Annie Leonard, Greenpeace USA Executive Director wrote:

> "We 'bear witnesses' to environmental destruction in a peaceful, non-violent manner. We use non-violent confrontation to raise the level and quality of public debate...We ensure our financial independence from political or commercial interests." Greenpeace challenges the systems of power and privilege that destroy the environment and place disproportionate burdens on vulnerable communities (Greenpeace's website).

Photo Image 6.6: Greenpeace
The Rainbow Warrior during Greenpeace activists protest on September 8, 2008, against Israel's plan to build a new electricity power plant fueled by coal in Ashkelon, Israel
Credit: ChameleonsEye/Shutterstock

Moreover, at the core of everything, Greenpeace is an idea: the idea that together, we can build a green and peaceful future in a way that is more equitable, sustainable and fair.

Arbor Day

From the Latin Arbor ~ *Meaning Tree*

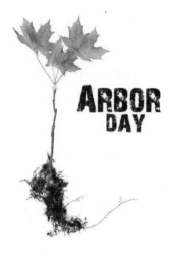

Arbor Day is celebrated across the globe, when individuals and groups are encouraged to plant and care for trees. The first documented arbor plantation festival took place in 1594, in The Spanish village of Mondoñedo, and it was organized by its mayor. Later, in 1805, the small Spanish village of Villanueva de la Sierra held the first modern Arbor Day. When the initiative was launched it was enthusiastically supported by the entire population (Herrero Uceda, 2011). The mayor was persuaded to act based on the knowledge of a local priest, don Ramón Vacas Roxo, who was convinced of the importance of trees for health, hygiene, decoration, nature, environment and customs. The tree celebration also gave a badly needed festive air to the town because at this point in history, Spain was under the threat of Napoleon, who was ravaging Europe and its land; therefore the idea to urgently plant trees was embraced.

Fun Fact: When Napoleon was proclaimed Emperor of the French in 1804, he wanted to break from tradition, thus choosing a unique emblem was important to him. The bee was among the many symbols he selected, because it was believed to be a symbol of immortality and resurrection.

In the Americas similar advocacy would occur. It has been recorded that the first American Arbor Day took place on April 10, 1872, in Nebraska City, Nebraska, and was instituted by J. Sterling Morton. He had been among the many pioneers who move into the Nebraska Territory in 1854. Morton and his wife had moved from Detroit, they were lovers of nature, and the home they established in Nebraska was quickly planted with trees, shrubs and flowers. Morton wrote, "Each generation takes the earth as trustees." Driven by Morton`s initiative it is estimated that on that very first Arbor Day; April 10, 1872, one million trees were planted in Nebraska.

In Canada, according to the Ontario Teachers' Manuals "History of Education" (1915), Arbour day was founded by Sir George W. Ross, when he was Minister of Education in Ontario (1883-1899). Ross would later become Premier of Ontario. Canada does not have one designated National Arbour Day. Canada's National Forest Week (The Canadian Forestry Association) is the last full week of September, and National Tree Day (Maple Leaf Day) falls on the Wednesday of that week. Ontario celebrates Arbour Week from the last Friday in April to the first Sunday in May. Prince Edward Island celebrates Arbour Day on the third Friday in May during Arbor Week.

Today, many countries observe this day to celebrate with friends and families and their eco-communities. Though usually observed in the spring, the date varies, depending on climate and suitable planting season. We now conclude our last chapter with a celebration of our planet by examining the inception and the person behind Earth Day.

Earth Day: April 22

Earth Day Canada's Mission Statement is: to inspire and supports people across Canada to connect with nature and build resilient communities.

1970s was the first year of a new decade, and it would mark the beginning of major social change in North America. The Beatles had released their final album and Jimi Hendrix had just died. In Canada, one of the most socially progressive Bills ever drafted was passed in 1969. *Bill 150* would decriminalize homosexuality and the use of contraception, and it began the process of allowing women in Canada the legal right to an abortion (Bake, 2013). In the United States, it was the height of the counterculture movement. The Vietnam War was intense and students all over the country were overwhelmingly protesting. Then on April 22, Wisconsin Senator Gaylord Nelson would set into motion what would become the modern environmental movement.

Gaylord Nelson wanted to send a strong message to the politicians in State and Federal Governments — a missive to tell them to wake-up, to do something ~ and act urgently. He and his supporters harnessed the energy of the emerging social consciousness that had been sweeping the country during of the 1960s. They channeled the strength of the anti-war rallies, and the women's and gay rights movements, by putting environmental concerns front and center. More than 20 million American demonstrated. Now each year on April 22, globally we celebrate Earth Day, as it has become the largest secular observance in the world, celebrated by more than a billion people every year. It is a day of action that challenges human behaviour and provokes individual and policy changes. Gaylord Nelson died in 2005 at the aged 89.

2020 will mark the **50th** anniversary of the First Earth Day
In honour of this milestone, *what might you do*?

CHAPTER REVIEW QUESTIONS

1. Which scientist was awarded the Nobel Prize in Physiology or Medicine?
   a. Paul Hermann Müller
   b. Karl von Frisch
   c. Senator Gaylord Nelson
   d. Johann Dzierzon

2. In what year was the first Earth Day Celebrated?
   a. 1965
   b. 1970
   c. 1972
   d. 1976

3. Which of the following books is credited with starting the environmental movement?
   a. The Noisy Summer
   b. The End of the Song Birds
   c. The Silent Spring
   d. Our Melting Glaciers

4. In what year was the ground breaking book noted in question #3 published?
   a. 1952
   b. 1962
   c. 1967
   d. 1972

5. In which year did Canada enact the original Canadian Environmental Protection Act?
   a. 1978
   b. 1985
   c. 1988
   d. 1995

6. Rachel Carson's work was rewarded by receiving all of the following EXCEPT which one?
   a. A USA stamp with her portrait
   b. A namesake for prizes awarded by philanthropic groups
   c. A Nobel Prize in Science and Biology
   d. The Presidential Medal of Freedom

7. In what city and country was the first Earth Day celebrated?
    a. Wisconsin, USA
    b. Vancouver, Canada
    c. Stockholm, Sweden
    d. Morges, Switzerland

8. In what country was the World Wildlife Fund first established?
    a. Canada
    b. Sweden
    c. Switzerland
    d. USA

9. Which best describes the number of years the World Wildlife Fund has been active?
    a. 20 years
    b. 30 years
    c. 40 years
    d. 50 years

10. Canada has a National Arbour Day each year.
    a. True
    b. False

ACTIVITIES

To enhance your understanding and nurture your curiosities check out the following:

I. Typhus in Ontario Canada
   - http://ontarioplaques.com/Plaques/Plaque_Frontenac22.html

II. The David Suzuki Foundation's website
   - http://www.davidsuzuki.org/about/

III. A documentary On the American experience: Rachel Carson
   - http://video.krwg.org/video/2365935530/

IV. What Really Happened - The Silent Spring Of Rachel Carson
   - https://www.youtube.com/watch?v=c6fAP6Fjx-Y

V. Documentary 2017 | Rachel Carson - The Life and Legacy; 2 hours
   - https://www.youtube.com/watch?v=vODO6m7ipPQ

VI. World Wild Life website
   - http://www.worldwildlife.org/about/history

KEY TERMS

Animate
- Bring to life

Ethos
- The spirit of a culture, era, or community as manifested in its beliefs and aspirations

DDT ~ dichloro-diphenyl-trichloroethane
- Was developed as the first of the modern synthetic insecticides in the 1940s
- Initially used to combat malaria, typhus, and the other insect-borne human diseases among both military and civilian populations

Dengue Fever
- Is a mosquito-borne flavivirus disease that has spread to most tropical and many subtropical areas (WHO)

Inanimate
- Not alive, especially not in the manner of animals and humans

Typhus
- Also known as typhus fever is a group of infectious diseases
- Common symptoms include fever, headache, and a rash

Water-insoluble
- In science, the term is used to describe substances with a low solubility.
- Solubility is the ability for a substance to dissolve when mixed with another substance to form a new compound

Review Time

1. What are the most important ideas generated?
2. Which part of the text led you to these insights?
3. How do you think these issues are viewed by others?

A. Can you draw a diagram to illustrate the Honey Bee's anatomy and;
B. Explain its function?

BIBLIOGRAPHY

Angel, H. (2016). *Pollination Power*. University of Chicago Press

Amdam, G. V. and Omholt, S. W. (2003). The hive bee to forager transition in honeybee colonies: the double repressor hypothesis. *Journal of Theoretical Biology, Vol 223*, Issue 4, 21, Pages 451–464.

Arteca, R. (2015). *Introduction to Horticultural* Science. 2nd Edition, Cengage Learning

Bake, A. (2013). *Intimate Personal Violence in Canada*. 1st Canadian Edition, Pearson

Barth Jr., R. H. (1969). Pheromone-endocrine interactions in insects. In: Benson GK, Phillips JG (eds). *Hormones and the environment*. Cambridge University Press, London, pp 373–404

Benyus, J. M. (1992). *Beastly Behaviors: A Watcher's Guide to How Animals Act and Why*. Addison-Wesley

Bignami. G. F. (2000). The microscope's coat of arms …or, the sting of the bee and the moons of Jupiter. *Nature Vol 405*

Blaauw, B. R., and Isaacs, R. (2014). Flower plantings increase wild bee abundance and the pollination services provided to a pollination-dependent crop. *Journal of Applied Ecology, 51*, 890–898

Blackiston, H. (2015). *Beekeeping for Dummies*. Wiley Brand

Blum, M.S. (1992). *Honey bee pheromones in The Hive and the Honey Bee*. Revised edition (Dadant and Sons: Hamilton, Illinois), pages 385–389.

Blocha, G., Francoyb, T. M., Wachtelc, I, Panitz-Cohenc, Fuchsd, S., and Mazarc, A. *Industrial apiculture in the Jordan valley during Biblical times with Anatolian honeybees* (2010). Edited by Bruce Smith, National Museum of Natural History, Smithsonian Institution, Washington, DC, Edited by Bruce Smith, National Museum of Natural History, Smithsonian Institution, Washington, DC, and approved May 10, 2010, retrieved on March 7, 2017 from http://www.pnas.org/content/107/25/11240http://www.pnas.org/content/107/25/11240

Boch, R., and Shearer, D.A. (1971). Chemical releasers of alarm behaviour on the honey-bee, Apis mellifera. *Journal of Insect Physiology 17*, 2277–2285.

Boes, K. E. (2009). Honeybee colony drone production and maintenance in accordance with environmental factors: An interplay of queen and worker decisions. *Insectes Sociaux 57*(1):1-9.

Briant, T. J. (1884), On the Anatomy and Functions of the Tongue of the Honey-Bee (Worker). *Journal of the Linnean Society of London, Zoology, 17*: 408–417. doi: 10.1111/j.1096-3642.1883.tb02033.x

Brodrick, (1972). *Animals in Archaeology*. Praeger, New York.

Brooks, P. (1972). *The House of Life: Rachel Carson at Work*. Houghton Mifflin. ISBN 0-395-13517-6. This book is a personal memoir by Carson's Houghton Mifflin editor and close friend Paul Brooks. Brooks' papers are housed at the Thoreau Institute at Walden Woods Library.

Buchmann, S. L. (2005). *Letters from the Hive: An Intimate History of Bees, Honey, and Humankind*. Bantam Books: New York.

Bujok, B., Kleinhenz, M., & Fuchs S, Tautz J. (2002). Hot spots in the bee hive. *Naturwissenschaften 89,* 299-301.

Butler, C. (1609). The Feminine Monarchie. On a Treatise Concerning Bees, and the Due Ordering of them. Joseph Barnes: Oxford.

Butler, C. (1608). The 'piping' and 'quacking' of queen bees" (Web Article). The Moir Rare Book Collection. National Library of Scotland. Retrieved 2008-01-08.

Byfield, M. (2000). Report / Newsmagazine (Alberta Edition). Vol. 26 Issue 47, p. 24.

Camazine, S. (1993). The regulation of pollen foraging by honey bees: how foragers assess the colony's need for pollen. *Behav. Ecol. Sociobiol. 32*: 265Ð272.

Casida, J. E., Quistad, G. B. (1998). Golden age of insecticide research: past, present, or future? *Annu. Rev. Entomol. 1998, 43,* 1-16. http://biomedical.AnnualReviews.org/

Christenhusz, M., Reveal, J., Farjon, A., Mill, R. R., and Chase, M. W. (2011). A new classification and linear sequence of extant gymnosperms. *Phytotaxa 19*: pgs. 55–70

Collins, A. M, and Rothenbuhler, W. C. (1978). Laboratory test of the response to an alarm chemical, isopentyl acetate, by Apis mellifera. *Ann Entomol Soc Am 71*:906–909 Google Scholar

Crane, E., (1990). *Bees and beekeeping: Science, practice, and world resources*. Ithaca, New York, Cornell University Press.

Croome, J. and Hatt, C. (2016). You asked, we answered: Why we're going to court to protect the bees. Ecojustice Blog. Retrieved on April 1, 2017, from https://www.ecojustice.ca/you-asked-we-answered-bees/.

Czekońska, K., Chuda-Mickiewicz, B. (2015). The ability of honey bee drones to ejaculate. *Journal of APIC. SCI. Vol. 59* No. 2 2015, pgs 127- 133.

Dade, A. D. (2009). Anatomy and Dissection of the Honey bee. Retrieved on March 25, 2017 from https://books.google.ca/books?id=_JEaMktVWEMC&pg=PA51&lpg=PA51&dq=honey+bee+sternites+plates+anatomy&source=bl&ots=MytkhEzL5S&sig=uUJY59Qqs82jmBwv63joiKPWHTE&hl=en&sa=X&ved=0ahUKEwjktauJmvLSAhXq44MKHQGEDOsQ6AEIQDAG#v=onepage&q=honey%20bee%20sternites%20plates%20anatomy&f=false

Dallai R. (1975). Fine structure of the spermatheca of Apis mellifera. *Journal of Insect Physiology, 21*, 89–109.

Darrach, M., and Page, S. (2016). Statistical Overview of the Canadian Honey and Bee Industry and the Economic Contribution of Honey Bee Pollination. Prepared by the Horticulture and Cross Sectoral DivisionAgriculture and Agri-Food Canada. Retrieved form http://www.agr.gc.ca/resources/prod/doc/pdf/1453219857143-eng.pdf

Delaplane, K.S. & Mayer, D.F. (2000) *Crop Pollination by Bees*. CABI Publishing, New York, NY, USA.

de la Croix, H., & Tansey, R. G. (1980). *Gardner's Art through the Ages*. Harcourt Brace Jovanovish Publishers, New York.

Doolittle, G. M. (1889). Scientific queen-rearing. T. Newman & Son, Chicago

Driessen, P. (2014). Perils of commercial beekeeping. Honeybees pollinate crops but endure stress, parasites, and disease. Solutions are coming. Retrieved on May 12, 2017, from http://www.cfact.org/2014/04/06/perils-of-commercial-beekeeping/

Dunckel, M. (2013). Small, medium, large – Does farm size really matter? Michigan University Retrieved on May 14, 2017, from http://msue.anr.msu.edu/news/small_medium_large_does_farm_size_really_matter.

Dunlap, T. (2014). *DDT: Scientists, Citizens, and Public Policy*. Princeton University Press. ISBN 978-1-4008-5385-4.

Dyer F.C. (2002). The biology of the dance language. *Annu Rev Entomol.*; *47*: 917- 49

Ellis, J. (2015). *The External Anatomy of the Honey Bee*. (Retrieved from The American Bee Journal on March 20, 2017 form http://americanbeejournal.com/the-components-of-a-honey-bee-nest/). Encyclopedia Britannica. retrieved on February 25, 2017 from https://www.britannica.com/science/eusocial-species

Environment Canada and the Ontario Ministry of the Environment (2011). Canada-Ontario Agreement, Respecting the Great Lakes Basin Ecosystem . 2007–2010 Progress Report Retrieved on May 24, 2017 from, http://publications.gc.ca/collections/collection_2012/ec/En161-5-2010-eng.pdf

Facklam, M. and Johnson. P. (1992). B*ees Dance and Whales Sing: The Mysteries of Animal Communication.* Published by the San Francisco Sierra Club.

Fahrbach, S., E., Giray, T., and Robinson, G. E. (1995). Volume changes in the Mushroom bodies of Adult Honey bee Queens. *Neurobiology of learning and memory, 63, 181-191.*

Free, J.B. (1993) *Insect Pollination of Crops*, 2nd edn, revised. Academic Press, San Diego, CA, USA.

Free, J. B, and Winder, M. E. (1983). Brood recognition by honey bee (Apis mellifera) workers. *Anim Behav 31*:539–545 Google Scholar

Free, J. B. (1987). *Pheromones of social bees.* Ithaca, N.Y.: Comstock.

Gallai, N., Salles, J., Settele, J. & Vaissiere, B. (2009) Economic valuation of the vulnerability of world agriculture confronted with pollinator decline. *Ecological Economics, 68*, 810–821.

Goras, G., Tananaki C., Gounari S., Lazaridou E., Kanelis D., Liolios V., Karazafiris E., Thrasyvoulou A. (2016). Rearing drones in queen cells of apis mellifera honey bees. J. APIC. SCI. VOL. 60 NO. Retrieved on March 23, 2017, retrieved from https://www.degruyter.com/downloadpdf/j/jas.2016.60.issue-2/jas-2016-0033/jas-2016-0033.pdf

Gould, J.L. and Gould, C.G. (1988). The Honeybee. Published by W. H. Freeman,.

Government of Canada (2013-2014). Agriculture and Agri-Food Canada (2013-2014). Statistical Overview of the Canadian Honey and Bee Industry and the Economic Contribution of Honey Bee Pollination Retrieved on May 12, 2017, retrieved from http://www.agr.gc.ca/eng/industry-markets-and-trade/statistics-and-market-information/by-product-sector/horticulture-industry/horticulture-sector-reports/statistical-overview-of-the-canadian-honey-and-bee-industry-and-the-economic-contribution-of-honey-bee-pollination-2013-2014/?id=1453219857143

Grens, K. (2015). Galileo's improvements to the microscope led to the first published observations using such an instrument. Apiarium, 1625. Retrieved on March 31, 2017 from http://www.the-scientist.com/?articles.view/articleNo/42263/title/Apiarium--1625/

Harbo, J. R. (1979). The rate of depletion of spermatozoa in the queen honey-bee spermathecal. *J. Apic. Res. 18*: 204-207.

Haydak, M.H. (1958). Do nurse bees recognize the sex of the larvae? *Science, 12 7*(3306), 1113. http://d x . d o i . o r g / 10 .112 6 / s c i e n c e .12 7. 3 3 0 6 .1113.

Heinberg, R. (1989). Memories and Visions of Paradise: Exploring the Universal Myth of a Lost Golden Age, Los Angeles, Calif.: Tarche. MISBN 0-87477-515-9.

Heisenberg, M. (1998). What Do the Mushroom Bodies Do for the Insect Brain? An Introduction, *Learn Mem. 1998 May; 5*(1): 1–10.

Herrero Uceda, Miguel (2011). Arbor Day (in Spanish). Quercus, nature review. Retrived on May 18, 2017 from https://en.wikipedia.org/wiki/Villanueva_de_la_Sierra.

Hornsey, I. (2003). The History of Beer and Brewing. The Royal Society of Chemistry. Retrieved on April 27, 2017 from https://books.google.ca/books?id=QqnvNsgas20C&printsec=frontcover&redir_esc=y&hl=en#v=onepage&q&f=false

Johnson, R. N., Oldroyd, B. P., Barron, A. B., and Crozier, R. H. (2002). Genetic Control of the Honey Bee (Apis mellifera) Dance Language: Segregating Dance Forms in a Backcrossed Colony. *The American Genetic Association 93:170–173.*

Katz, N. and A. Ragoo. 2013. Statistical Overview of the Canadian Honey Industry, 2012. Agriculture and Agri-Food Canada.

Kenyon, F. C. (1896). The brain of the bee—A preliminary contribution to the morphology of the nervous system of the Arthropoda. *J Comp Neurol.;6*:134–210.

Kessler, R., and Harley, M. (206). Pollen. *The Hidden Sexuality of Flowers.* Earth Aware Edition.

Kevan PG, and Eisikowitch D. (1990). The effects of insect pollination on canola (Brassica napus L. cv. O.A.C. Triton) seed germination. Euphytica 45:39–41

Klein, A.M., Vaissiere, E.B., Cane, J.H., Steffan-Dewenter, I., Cunningham, S.A., Kremen, C. & Tscharntke, T. (2007) Importance of pollinators in changing landscapes for world crops. Proceedings of the *Royal Society B, 274,* 303–313.

Langstroth, L. L. (1860). *A Practical Treaties on the Hive and the Honey-bee.* 3rd edition, Northern Bee Books, Scout Bottom Farm, Mytholmroyd

Larson, K. (2007). "Bad Blood". On Earth. Retrieved on March 14, 2017 from http://archive.onearth.org/article/bad-blood

Lear, L. (1997). *Rachel Carson: Witness for Nature*. New York: Henry Holt. ISBN 0-8050-3428-5.

Linghu Z., Wu J., Wang C., Yan S. (2015). Mouthpart grooming behavior in honeybees: Kinematics and sectionalized friction between foreleg tarsi and proboscises. *Journal of insect physiology, Vol, 82*. Pages 122–128

Longnecker M.P., Rogan, W.J., Lucier, G. (1997).The Human Health effects of DDT (DICHLORODIPHENYLTRICHLOROETHANE) and PCBS (POLYCHLORINATED BIPHENYLS) and an overview of organochlorines in public health. Annual Review of Public *Health, Vol. 18*:211-244.

Maisto, S., Galizio, M., Connors, G.J., Maheu, S., and McCarthy, A. (2013). *Drug Use and Abuse*. Nelson Education.

Mangum, W. A. (2015), retrieved on April 3, 2017 from http://americanbeejournal.com/u-s-queen-rearing-history/

Mandal, M.D., and Mandal, S. (2011). Asian Pac J Trop Biomed. *Apr; 1(2):* 154–160. Retrieved on March 11, 2017, from https://www.ncbi.nlm.nih.gov/pmc/articles/PMC3609166/

Manning, R. and J. Boland. 2000. A preliminary investigation into honey bee (Apis mellifera) pollination of canola (Brassica napus cv. Karoo) in Western Australia. Australian Journal of Experimental Agriculture. *Vol. 40, No. 3*: 439-442

Martin, E. C. (1980). Beekeeping in America. The United States Department of Agriculture. Retrived on March 13, 2017, from https://naldc.nal.usda.gov/download/CAT81750530/PDF

Mazar A. and Panitz-Cohen, N. (2007). It Is the Land of Honey: Beekeeping at Tel Rehov. Retrieved on March 31, 2017, from http://www.rehov.org/Rehov/publications/Mazar_NEA70_4.pdf

McBrayer, Z., Ono, H., Shimell, MJ., Parvy, JP., Beckstead, R.B., Warren, J.T., Thummel, C.S., Dauphin-Villemant , C., Lawrence, G., and O'Connor, M. B. (2008). Prothoracicotropic hormone regulates developmental timing and body size in Drosophila. Dev Cell.,13(6): 857–871. Retrieved on March 13, 2017, received from https://www.ncbi.nlm.nih.gov/pmc/articles/PMC2359579/

McKay, A., Herold, E. S., Nevid, J. S., Fichner-Rathus, L., and Rathus S. A. (2015). Human Sexuality in a World of Diversity. 5th Canadian Edition. Pearson Education. Toronto

Molan, P.C. (1997). *"Honey as an Antimicrobial Agent." Bee Products: Properties, Applications, and Apitherapy*. Plenum Press: New York and London.

Moritz, R.F.A. and Burgin, H. (1987). Group response to alarm pheromones in socialwasps and the honeybees. *Ethology 76*, 15–26.

Murphy, P. (2005). What a Book Can Do: The Publication and Reception of Silent Spring. Amherst: University of Massachusetts Press. ISBN 978-1-55849-582-1.

Neumann, P. & Carreck, N.L. (2010) Honey bee colony losses. *Journal of Apiculture Research, 49*, 1–6.

Oldroyd, B. P. (2007). "What's Killing American Honey Bees?". PLoS Biology. 5 (6): e168. doi:10.1371/journal.pbio.0050168. PMC 1892840Freely accessible. PMID 17564497.

Palmer, J. D., Soltis, D. E., and Chase, M. W. (2004). The plant tree of life: An overview and some points of view. *The American Journal of Botany, 29*. Retrieved on April 13, 2017 from http://www.amjbot.org/content/91/10/1437.ful

Pankiw T, and Rubink W. L. (2002). Pollen foraging response to brood pheromone by Africanized and European honey bees (Apis mellifera L.) *Ann Entomol Soc Am, 95*:761–767.

Pesticide action network (2017). The DDT Story. Retrieved on April 1, 2017, form http://www.panna.org/resources/ddt-story

Raghavan, V. (1997). Molecular Embryology of Flowering Plants. Cambridge University Press. pp. 210–216. ISBN 978-0-521-55246-2.

Readicker-Henderson, E. (2009). *A Short History of the Honey Bee: Humans, Flowers, and Bees in the Eternal Chase for Honey.* Timber Press

Roberson, R. (2016). Enlightened Piety during the Age of Benevolence: The Christian Knowledge Movement in the British Atlantic World", *Church History, 85* (2): 246,

Root, A.I., and Root, E.R. (1980). *The ABC and Xyz of Bee Culture*. Medina, Ohio: A.I. Root. OCLC 6586488.

Ross, D. (2015). The Dissolution of the Monasteries. Retrieved on April 10, 2017, from http://www.britainexpress.com/History/Dissolution_of_the_Monasteries.htm

Rueppell, O., Bachelier, C., Fondrk, M. K. and Page, R. E. (2007). Regulation of life history determines lifespan of worker honey bees (Apis mellifera L.). *Experimental Gerontology*; *42*(10): pgs., 1020–1032. Retrieved on March 13, 2017 from, https://www.ncbi.nlm.nih.gov/pmc/articles/PMC2398712/

Saunders, E. (1907). *Wild bees, wasps and ants.* Dutton and Company, New York.

Seeley, T. (1996). *Wisdom of the Hive*. Harvard University Press. ISBN 978-0-674-95376-5.

Seeley, T. D. (1985). *Honeybee ecology: a study of adaptation in social life*. Princeton University Press, Princeton.

Seeley, T. D. (2010). *Honeybee Democracy*. Princeton University Press. New Jersey

Shukla, A. K, Vijayaraghavan, M. R., and Chaudhry, B. (1998). "Abiotic pollination". Biology Of Pollen. Retrieved on May 3, 2017, from
https://books.google.ca/books?id=jfSlwa0BnDgC&pg=PA67&redir_esc=y#v=onepage&q&f=false

Smith, J. (1949). *Better Queens*. Retrieved on March 5, 2017 from
http://www.bushfarms.com/beesbetterqueens.htm

Stell, I., M. (2012). Retrieved on March 6, 2017 at http://www.understandingbeeanatomy.com/wp-content/uploads/2012/10/Chapter-9-The-Respiratory-System2.pdf

Snodgrass, R. E. (1956). *Anatomy of the honey bee*. Comstock Publishing Associates, Ithaca.

Tew, J. E. (2015). *The Beekeeper's Problem Solver*. Quid Publishing.

Thom, C., Gilley, D.C., Hooper, J, and Esch, H. E. (2007). The Scent of the Waggle Dance. *PLoS Biol. Sep; 5*(9): e228

Underwood, R.M.; Lewis, M.J., and Hare, J.F. (2004). Reduced worker relatedness does not affect cooperation in honey bee colonies. *Canadian Journal of Zoology. Vol. 82* Issue 9, pgs. 1542-1545. 4p.

vanEngelsdorp, D., Cox-Foster, D., Frazier, M., Ostiguy, N., and Hayes, J. (2006). "Colony Collapse Disorder Preliminary Report" (PDF). Mid-Atlantic Apiculture Research and Extension Consortium (MAAREC) – CCD Working Group. p. 22. Retrieved 2007-04-24.
http://www.apiservices.biz/en/articles/sort-by-popularity/492-colony-collapse-disorder-ccdferences

vanEngelsdorp, D., Evans, J. D, Saegerman, C., Mullin, C., Haubruge, E., Nguyen, B.K., Frazier, M., Frazier, J., Cox-Foster, D., Chen, Y., Underwood. R., Tarpy, D. R., and Pettis, J. S. (2009). Colony Collapse Disorder: A Descriptive Study. Journal.pone.0006481. Retrieved on April 9, 2017, retrieved from http://journals.plos.org/plosone/article?id=10.1371/journal.pone.0006481

Velthuis H.H.W. (1970). Ovarian development in Apis mellifera worker bees. *Entomologia Experimentalis et Applicata 13*. Pgs. 377–394.

Visscher, P.K, Dukas R. (1997). Survivorship of foraging honey bees. *Ins Soc., 44*:1–5.

Voeller, D. & Nieh, J. (2009). Aggressive reaction level of the honeybee (apis mellifera l.) to smell and knock. *Journal of Apicultural Science Vol. 53* No. 1. Retrieved from,
http://www.jas.org.pl/pdf/186.pdf

von Frisch, K. (1963). *The Dancing Bees: An Account of the Life and Senses of the Honeybee*. Published by Harcourt, Brace. Methuen

Warton, K. E., Dryer, F., Yong Huang, Z., and Getty, T. (2007). The honeybee queen influences the regulation of colony drone production. *Behavioral Ecology 18*(6): pgs., 1092-1099.

Watson P. (1981). Sea Shepherd: My Fight for Whales and Seals ISBN 0-393-01499-1

Wilkes, D. (2011). The real queen bees at Buck House: A unique insight into Her Majesty's favourite honey - made in her own backyard. *The Daily News*. Retrieved on March 12, 2017, from http://www.dailymail.co.uk/news/article-2028696/A-unique-insight-Her-Majestys-favourite-honey--backyard.html

Winesmarch, M. (2013). Mystery Malady Kills More Bees, Heightening Worry on Farms http://www.nytimes.com/2013/03/29/science/earth/soaring-bee-deaths-in-2012-sound-alarm-on-malady.html

Winston, M.L. (1987). *The Biology of the Honey bee.* Harvard University Press, Cambridge, Massachusetts London England.

Winston, M.L. (2014). *Bee Time. Lessons from the Hive*. Harvard University Press.

Wilson-Rich, N. (2014). *The Bee; A Natural History*. Princeton University Press.

World Health Organization (1979). DDT and its derivatives, Environmental Health Criteria monograph No. 009, Geneva: World Health Organization, ISBN 92-4-154069-9. Retrieved on March 14, 2017, from http://www.inchem.org/documents/ehc/ehc/ehc009.htm

Younger, W. (1966). *Gods, Men and Wine*. London, 1966. AbeBooks